**TEACHER'S PET PUBLICATIONS**

# PUZZLE PACK
## for
## Hiroshima

based on the book by
John Hersey

Written by
William T. Collins

© 2005 Teacher's Pet Publications
All Rights Reserved

The materials in this packet are copyrighted
by Teacher's Pet Publications, Inc.

These pages may be duplicated by the purchaser
for use in the purchaser's own classroom.

Copying any of these materials and distributing them
for any other purpose is a violation of the copyright laws.

© 2005 Teacher's Pet Publications, Inc.
www.tpet.com

## INTRODUCTION
If you already own the LitPlan for this title, this Puzzle Pack will refresh your Unit Resource Materials and Vocabulary Resource Materials sections plus give you additional materials you can substitute into the tests. If you do not already have a complete LitPlan, these pages will give you some supplemental materials to use with your own plan. There are two main groups of materials: one set for unit words (such as characters' names, symbols, places, etc.) and one set for vocabulary words associated with the book.

## WORD LIST
There is a word list for both the unit words and the vocabulary words. These lists show you which words are being used in the materials and the clues or definitions being used for those words. You may want to give students a word list with clues/definitions to help them, or you may want students to only have a word list (without clues/definitions) if you want them to work a little harder. Both are available for duplication. The word lists can also be your "calling key" for the bingo games.

## FILL IN THE BLANK AND MATCHING
There are 4 each of the fill in the blank and matching worksheets for both the unit and vocabulary words. These pages can be used either as extra worksheets for students or as objective parts of a unit test. They can be done individually if students need extra help or as a whole class activity to review the material covered.

## MAGIC SQUARES
The magic squares not only reinforce the material covered but also work on reasoning and math skills. Many teachers have told us that their students really enjoy doing these!

## WORD SEARCH PUZZLES
The word search words go in all directions, as indicated on your answer keys. Two of the word search puzzles have the clues listed rather than the words. This makes the puzzle a little more difficult, but it reinforces the material better. Two word search puzzles have words only for students who find the clue puzzles too difficult.

## CROSSWORD PUZZLES
Both unit and vocabulary word sections have 4 crossword puzzles.

## BINGO CARDS
There are 32 individual bingo cards for the unit words and 32 individual bingo cards for the vocabulary words. You can use your word list as a "call list," calling the words at random and marking them off of your list as you go, or you could use the flash cards by cutting them apart and drawing the words at random from a hat (or box or whatever). To make a better review, you might ask for the definition and spelling of each word as you call it out–or you could call out the definitions and have students tell you the words they need to look for on the puzzle.

## JUGGLE LETTERS
The vocabulary juggle letter game is intended to help students learn the spellings of the words. One sheet has the definitions listed on it as an extra help for students who need it or to reinforce the definitions if you choose to do so.

## FLASH CARDS
We've included a set of vocabulary flash cards you can duplicate, cut, and fold for your students. Some teachers make a few sets for general use by the class; others make a set for each student. Some teachers duplicate them for each student and have the students cut & fold their own. You can cut out just the words and put them in a hat, have each student pick out one word and write the definition and a sentence for that word. Students then swap words and papers, with the next student adding a sentence of his own under the last one. You can have students swap as many times as you like. Each time the student will read the sentences written prior to his own and then add a sentence. You can cut out the words and definitions separately and play "I Have; Who Has?" Each student in the room draws a word and definition. The first student says, "I have (the name of the word). Who has the definition?" The student with the definition reads it then says, "I have (the name of the vocabulary word she has). Who has the definition?" The round continues until all words and definitions have been given.

## Hiroshima Word List

| No. | Word | Clue/Definition |
|---|---|---|
| 1. | AMERICANS | They dropped the bombs. |
| 2. | ASANO | ___ Park |
| 3. | ATOMIC | Kind of bombs dropped on Japan |
| 4. | BLOOD | These disorders are common in the second stages of radiation sickness. |
| 5. | BOMBS | Two were dropped on Japan. |
| 6. | CLERK | Saski's occupation |
| 7. | DOCTOR | Fujii's occupation |
| 8. | DUST | Kind of cloud in Hiroshima after the bomb |
| 9. | EXPLOSION | There was no sound of an ___ when the bomb went off. |
| 10. | FAN | Shape of the city of Hiroshima |
| 11. | FIRES | The bombs caused these & winds blew them out of control. |
| 12. | FUJII | Doctor who owned & operated a private hospital |
| 13. | HAIR | One symptom of radiation sickness: ___ falls out |
| 14. | HERSEY | Author |
| 15. | HIBAKUSHA | Explosion-affected persons |
| 16. | HIROSHIMA | City on which 1st bomb was dropped |
| 17. | HOSPITALS | Short-staffed, over-crowded places after the bombing |
| 18. | JAPAN | Country in which Hiroshima is located |
| 19. | KLEINSORGE | German priest |
| 20. | KYO | River near Asano Park |
| 21. | LEUKEMIA | Blood disease common among survivors |
| 22. | LIGHT | People saw a bright ___ when the bomb went off. |
| 23. | MR | Nickname for the B29 bombers: ___. B |
| 24. | NAGASAKI | City on which 2nd bomb was dropped |
| 25. | NAKAMURA | Tailor's widow with small children |
| 26. | NUN | Saski eventually became one |
| 27. | PARK | Asano ___ |
| 28. | PASTOR | Tanimoto's occupation |
| 29. | RADIATION | People suffered from ___ sickness & burns. |
| 30. | RICE | Staple food |
| 31. | RIVERS | Waterways of Hiroshima |
| 32. | SASAKI | Doctor at Red Cross hospital; became wealthy |
| 33. | SASKI | Clerk at East Asia Tin Works trapped under bookcases |
| 34. | SEWING | Mrs. Nakamura's ___ machine rusted in her well. |
| 35. | SIREN | Warning sound telling people to go to safe areas |
| 36. | SLIGHTLY | East Parade Ground doctor's first duty was to take care of the ___ wounded |
| 37. | SPAS | Sasaki built these. |
| 38. | TANIMOTO | Pastor of Hiroshima Methodist Church |
| 39. | WATER | People drank contaminated ___. |

Hiroshima Fill In The Blanks 1

_____

_____

_____

_____

_____

_____

_____

_____

_____

_____

_____

_____

_____

_____

_____

_____

_____

_____

_____

_____

1. Blood disease common among survivors
2. These disorders are common in the second stages of radiation sickness.
3. Author
4. People drank contaminated ___.
5. City on which 2nd bomb was dropped
6. ___ Park
7. East Parade Ground doctor's first duty was to take care of the ___ wounded
8. River near Asano Park
9. People saw a bright ___ when the bomb went off.
10. Tailor's widow with small children
11. Two were dropped on Japan.
12. Pastor of Hiroshima Methodist Church
13. Shape of the city of Hiroshima
14. Mrs. Nakamura's ___ machine rusted in her well.
15. Doctor at Red Cross hospital; became wealthy
16. Staple food
17. They dropped the bombs.
18. One symptom of radiation sickness: ___ falls out
19. Doctor who owned & operated a private hospital
20. The bombs caused these & winds blew them out of control.

Hiroshima Fill In The Blanks 1 Answer Key

| | |
|---|---|
| LEUKEMIA | 1. Blood disease common among survivors |
| BLOOD | 2. These disorders are common in the second stages of radiation sickness. |
| HERSEY | 3. Author |
| WATER | 4. People drank contaminated ___. |
| NAGASAKI | 5. City on which 2nd bomb was dropped |
| ASANO | 6. ___ Park |
| SLIGHTLY | 7. East Parade Ground doctor's first duty was to take care of the ___ wounded |
| KYO | 8. River near Asano Park |
| LIGHT | 9. People saw a bright ___ when the bomb went off. |
| NAKAMURA | 10. Tailor's widow with small children |
| BOMBS | 11. Two were dropped on Japan. |
| TANIMOTO | 12. Pastor of Hiroshima Methodist Church |
| FAN | 13. Shape of the city of Hiroshima |
| SEWING | 14. Mrs. Nakamura's ___ machine rusted in her well. |
| SASAKI | 15. Doctor at Red Cross hospital; became wealthy |
| RICE | 16. Staple food |
| AMERICANS | 17. They dropped the bombs. |
| HAIR | 18. One symptom of radiation sickness: ___ falls out |
| FUJII | 19. Doctor who owned & operated a private hospital |
| FIRES | 20. The bombs caused these & winds blew them out of control. |

Hiroshima Fill In The Blanks 2

_____

1. City on which 1st bomb was dropped
2. People suffered from ___ sickness & burns.
3. They dropped the bombs.
4. Explosion-affected persons
5. Kind of bombs dropped on Japan
6. Fujii's occupation
7. Two were dropped on Japan.
8. Sasaki built these.
9. People drank contaminated ___.
10. Blood disease common among survivors
11. Kind of cloud in Hiroshima after the bomb
12. One symptom of radiation sickness: ___ falls out
13. Country in which Hiroshima is located
14. Tailor's widow with small children
15. Doctor at Red Cross hospital; became wealthy
16. German priest
17. East Parade Ground doctor's first duty was to take care of the ___ wounded
18. Saski eventually became one
19. Mrs. Nakamura's ___ machine rusted in her well.
20. Tanimoto's occupation

Hiroshima Fill In The Blanks 2 Answer Key

| | |
|---|---|
| HIROSHIMA | 1. City on which 1st bomb was dropped |
| RADIATION | 2. People suffered from ___ sickness & burns. |
| AMERICANS | 3. They dropped the bombs. |
| HIBAKUSHA | 4. Explosion-affected persons |
| ATOMIC | 5. Kind of bombs dropped on Japan |
| DOCTOR | 6. Fujii's occupation |
| BOMBS | 7. Two were dropped on Japan. |
| SPAS | 8. Sasaki built these. |
| WATER | 9. People drank contaminated ___. |
| LEUKEMIA | 10. Blood disease common among survivors |
| DUST | 11. Kind of cloud in Hiroshima after the bomb |
| HAIR | 12. One symptom of radiation sickness: ___ falls out |
| JAPAN | 13. Country in which Hiroshima is located |
| NAKAMURA | 14. Tailor's widow with small children |
| SASAKI | 15. Doctor at Red Cross hospital; became wealthy |
| KLEINSORGE | 16. German priest |
| SLIGHTLY | 17. East Parade Ground doctor's first duty was to take care of the ___ wounded |
| NUN | 18. Saski eventually became one |
| SEWING | 19. Mrs. Nakamura's ___ machine rusted in her well. |
| PASTOR | 20. Tanimoto's occupation |

Hiroshima Fill In The Blanks 3

_____
_____
_____
_____
_____
_____
_____
_____
_____
_____
_____
_____
_____
_____
_____
_____
_____
_____
_____
_____

1. Saski eventually became one
2. Staple food
3. They dropped the bombs.
4. Pastor of Hiroshima Methodist Church
5. People suffered from ___ sickness & burns.
6. German priest
7. Author
8. People drank contaminated ___.
9. Two were dropped on Japan.
10. City on which 1st bomb was dropped
11. ___ Park
12. Warning sound telling people to go to safe areas
13. City on which 2nd bomb was dropped
14. There was no sound of an ___ when the bomb went off.
15. People saw a bright ___ when the bomb went off.
16. Doctor at Red Cross hospital; became wealthy
17. Kind of cloud in Hiroshima after the bomb
18. Country in which Hiroshima is located
19. Blood disease common among survivors
20. Shape of the city of Hiroshima

Hiroshima Fill In The Blanks 3 Answer Key

| | |
|---|---|
| NUN | 1. Saski eventually became one |
| RICE | 2. Staple food |
| AMERICANS | 3. They dropped the bombs. |
| TANIMOTO | 4. Pastor of Hiroshima Methodist Church |
| RADIATION | 5. People suffered from ___ sickness & burns. |
| KLEINSORGE | 6. German priest |
| HERSEY | 7. Author |
| WATER | 8. People drank contaminated ___. |
| BOMBS | 9. Two were dropped on Japan. |
| HIROSHIMA | 10. City on which 1st bomb was dropped |
| ASANO | 11. ___ Park |
| SIREN | 12. Warning sound telling people to go to safe areas |
| NAGASAKI | 13. City on which 2nd bomb was dropped |
| EXPLOSION | 14. There was no sound of an ___ when the bomb went off. |
| LIGHT | 15. People saw a bright ___ when the bomb went off. |
| SASAKI | 16. Doctor at Red Cross hospital; became wealthy |
| DUST | 17. Kind of cloud in Hiroshima after the bomb |
| JAPAN | 18. Country in which Hiroshima is located |
| LEUKEMIA | 19. Blood disease common among survivors |
| FAN | 20. Shape of the city of Hiroshima |

Hiroshima Fill In The Blanks 4

1. Pastor of Hiroshima Methodist Church
2. Saski's occupation
3. Staple food
4. ___ Park
5. East Parade Ground doctor's first duty was to take care of the ___ wounded
6. Shape of the city of Hiroshima
7. Short-staffed, over-crowded places after the bombing
8. There was no sound of an ___ when the bomb went off.
9. Mrs. Nakamura's ___ machine rusted in her well.
10. Kind of bombs dropped on Japan
11. Explosion-affected persons
12. Asano ___
13. Two were dropped on Japan.
14. Warning sound telling people to go to safe areas
15. The bombs caused these & winds blew them out of control.
16. Author
17. They dropped the bombs.
18. People saw a bright ___ when the bomb went off.
19. German priest
20. Waterways of Hiroshima

Hiroshima Fill In The Blanks 4 Answer Key

| | |
|---|---|
| TANIMOTO | 1. Pastor of Hiroshima Methodist Church |
| CLERK | 2. Saski's occupation |
| RICE | 3. Staple food |
| ASANO | 4. ___ Park |
| SLIGHTLY | 5. East Parade Ground doctor's first duty was to take care of the ___ wounded |
| FAN | 6. Shape of the city of Hiroshima |
| HOSPITALS | 7. Short-staffed, over-crowded places after the bombing |
| EXPLOSION | 8. There was no sound of an ___ when the bomb went off. |
| SEWING | 9. Mrs. Nakamura's ___ machine rusted in her well. |
| ATOMIC | 10. Kind of bombs dropped on Japan |
| HIBAKUSHA | 11. Explosion-affected persons |
| PARK | 12. Asano ___ |
| BOMBS | 13. Two were dropped on Japan. |
| SIREN | 14. Warning sound telling people to go to safe areas |
| FIRES | 15. The bombs caused these & winds blew them out of control. |
| HERSEY | 16. Author |
| AMERICANS | 17. They dropped the bombs. |
| LIGHT | 18. People saw a bright ___ when the bomb went off. |
| KLEINSORGE | 19. German priest |
| RIVERS | 20. Waterways of Hiroshima |

Hiroshima Matching 1

___ 1. PASTOR            A. ___ Park
___ 2. RICE              B. Kind of bombs dropped on Japan
___ 3. CLERK             C. Saski's occupation
___ 4. HOSPITALS         D. One symptom of radiation sickness: ___ falls out
___ 5. RIVERS            E. Waterways of Hiroshima
___ 6. EXPLOSION         F. Two were dropped on Japan.
___ 7. SASAKI            G. Staple food
___ 8. FAN               H. Kind of cloud in Hiroshima after the bomb
___ 9. KYO               I. German priest
___ 10. AMERICANS        J. Shape of the city of Hiroshima
___ 11. FUJII            K. River near Asano Park
___ 12. BOMBS            L. Tanimoto's occupation
___ 13. BLOOD            M. People saw a bright ___ when the bomb went off.
___ 14. ASANO            N. Pastor of Hiroshima Methodist Church
___ 15. SEWING           O. Short-staffed, over-crowded places after the bombing
___ 16. NAKAMURA         P. Tailor's widow with small children
___ 17. SIREN            Q. Doctor at Red Cross hospital; became wealthy
___ 18. KLEINSORGE       R. Asano ___
___ 19. ATOMIC           S. These disorders are common in the second stages of radiation sickness.
___ 20. TANIMOTO         T. Fujii's occupation
___ 21. HAIR             U. They dropped the bombs.
___ 22. LIGHT            V. Doctor who owned & operated a private hospital
___ 23. DUST             W. Warning sound telling people to go to safe areas
___ 24. DOCTOR           X. There was no sound of an ___ when the bomb went off.
___ 25. PARK             Y. Mrs. Nakamura's ___ machine rusted in her well.

Hiroshima Matching 1 Answer Key

| | | |
|---|---|---|
| L - 1. PASTOR | A. ___ Park |
| G - 2. RICE | B. Kind of bombs dropped on Japan |
| C - 3. CLERK | C. Saski's occupation |
| O - 4. HOSPITALS | D. One symptom of radiation sickness: ___ falls out |
| E - 5. RIVERS | E. Waterways of Hiroshima |
| X - 6. EXPLOSION | F. Two were dropped on Japan. |
| Q - 7. SASAKI | G. Staple food |
| J - 8. FAN | H. Kind of cloud in Hiroshima after the bomb |
| K - 9. KYO | I. German priest |
| U - 10. AMERICANS | J. Shape of the city of Hiroshima |
| V - 11. FUJII | K. River near Asano Park |
| F - 12. BOMBS | L. Tanimoto's occupation |
| S - 13. BLOOD | M. People saw a bright ___ when the bomb went off. |
| A - 14. ASANO | N. Pastor of Hiroshima Methodist Church |
| Y - 15. SEWING | O. Short-staffed, over-crowded places after the bombing |
| P - 16. NAKAMURA | P. Tailor's widow with small children |
| W - 17. SIREN | Q. Doctor at Red Cross hospital; became wealthy |
| I - 18. KLEINSORGE | R. Asano ___ |
| B - 19. ATOMIC | S. These disorders are common in the second stages of radiation sickness. |
| N - 20. TANIMOTO | T. Fujii's occupation |
| D - 21. HAIR | U. They dropped the bombs. |
| M - 22. LIGHT | V. Doctor who owned & operated a private hospital |
| H - 23. DUST | W. Warning sound telling people to go to safe areas |
| T - 24. DOCTOR | X. There was no sound of an ___ when the bomb went off. |
| R - 25. PARK | Y. Mrs. Nakamura's ___ machine rusted in her well. |

Hiroshima Matching 2

___ 1. JAPAN  A. ___ Park
___ 2. LEUKEMIA  B. People saw a bright ___ when the bomb went off.
___ 3. WATER  C. Shape of the city of Hiroshima
___ 4. FAN  D. Saski eventually became one
___ 5. LIGHT  E. Nickname for the B29 bombers: ___. B
___ 6. HERSEY  F. They dropped the bombs.
___ 7. AMERICANS  G. There was no sound of an ___ when the bomb went off.
___ 8. ASANO  H. Waterways of Hiroshima
___ 9. RIVERS  I. Warning sound telling people to go to safe areas
___ 10. EXPLOSION  J. Fujii's occupation
___ 11. DOCTOR  K. Blood disease common among survivors
___ 12. PARK  L. Asano ___
___ 13. CLERK  M. Kind of cloud in Hiroshima after the bomb
___ 14. SIREN  N. Tanimoto's occupation
___ 15. NUN  O. Sasaki built these.
___ 16. DUST  P. East Parade Ground doctor's first duty was to take care of the ___ wounded
___ 17. NAGASAKI  Q. One symptom of radiation sickness: ___ falls out
___ 18. HIBAKUSHA  R. City on which 2nd bomb was dropped
___ 19. SLIGHTLY  S. Saski's occupation
___ 20. SPAS  T. People suffered from ___ sickness & burns.
___ 21. SASKI  U. Explosion-affected persons
___ 22. MR  V. Author
___ 23. HAIR  W. People drank contaminated ___.
___ 24. RADIATION  X. Clerk at East Asia Tin Works trapped under bookcases
___ 25. PASTOR  Y. Country in which Hiroshima is located

Hiroshima Matching 2 Answer Key

| | |
|---|---|
| Y - 1. JAPAN | A. ___ Park |
| K - 2. LEUKEMIA | B. People saw a bright ___ when the bomb went off. |
| W - 3. WATER | C. Shape of the city of Hiroshima |
| C - 4. FAN | D. Saski eventually became one |
| B - 5. LIGHT | E. Nickname for the B29 bombers: ___. B |
| V - 6. HERSEY | F. They dropped the bombs. |
| F - 7. AMERICANS | G. There was no sound of an ___ when the bomb went off. |
| A - 8. ASANO | H. Waterways of Hiroshima |
| H - 9. RIVERS | I. Warning sound telling people to go to safe areas |
| G - 10. EXPLOSION | J. Fujii's occupation |
| J - 11. DOCTOR | K. Blood disease common among survivors |
| L - 12. PARK | L. Asano ___ |
| S - 13. CLERK | M. Kind of cloud in Hiroshima after the bomb |
| I - 14. SIREN | N. Tanimoto's occupation |
| D - 15. NUN | O. Sasaki built these. |
| M - 16. DUST | P. East Parade Ground doctor's first duty was to take care of the ___ wounded |
| R - 17. NAGASAKI | Q. One symptom of radiation sickness: ___ falls out |
| U - 18. HIBAKUSHA | R. City on which 2nd bomb was dropped |
| P - 19. SLIGHTLY | S. Saski's occupation |
| O - 20. SPAS | T. People suffered from ___ sickness & burns. |
| X - 21. SASKI | U. Explosion-affected persons |
| E - 22. MR | V. Author |
| Q - 23. HAIR | W. People drank contaminated ___. |
| T - 24. RADIATION | X. Clerk at East Asia Tin Works trapped under bookcases |
| N - 25. PASTOR | Y. Country in which Hiroshima is located |

Hiroshima Matching 3

___ 1. FUJII           A. Saski eventually became one
___ 2. SPAS            B. Country in which Hiroshima is located
___ 3. AMERICANS       C. Nickname for the B29 bombers: __. B
___ 4. FAN             D. Doctor who owned & operated a private hospital
___ 5. NAGASAKI        E. Staple food
___ 6. RICE            F. Tanimoto's occupation
___ 7. RADIATION       G. Shape of the city of Hiroshima
___ 8. SEWING          H. One symptom of radiation sickness: ___ falls out
___ 9. KYO             I. Sasaki built these.
___10. FIRES           J. Saski's occupation
___11. NUN             K. ___ Park
___12. HERSEY          L. People suffered from ___ sickness & burns.
___13. NAKAMURA        M. River near Asano Park
___14. SASAKI          N. The bombs caused these & winds blew them out of control.
___15. BOMBS           O. Two were dropped on Japan.
___16. TANIMOTO        P. Doctor at Red Cross hospital; became wealthy
___17. HAIR            Q. City on which 2nd bomb was dropped
___18. RIVERS          R. Explosion-affected persons
___19. JAPAN           S. They dropped the bombs.
___20. CLERK           T. Pastor of Hiroshima Methodist Church
___21. HIBAKUSHA       U. Author
___22. ASANO           V. People drank contaminated ___.
___23. PASTOR          W. Waterways of Hiroshima
___24. MR              X. Tailor's widow with small children
___25. WATER           Y. Mrs. Nakamura's ___ machine rusted in her well.

Hiroshima Matching 3 Answer Key

| | | |
|---|---|---|
| D - 1. FUJII | A. | Saski eventually became one |
| I - 2. SPAS | B. | Country in which Hiroshima is located |
| S - 3. AMERICANS | C. | Nickname for the B29 bombers: ___. B |
| G - 4. FAN | D. | Doctor who owned & operated a private hospital |
| Q - 5. NAGASAKI | E. | Staple food |
| E - 6. RICE | F. | Tanimoto's occupation |
| L - 7. RADIATION | G. | Shape of the city of Hiroshima |
| Y - 8. SEWING | H. | One symptom of radiation sickness: ___ falls out |
| M - 9. KYO | I. | Sasaki built these. |
| N -10. FIRES | J. | Saski's occupation |
| A -11. NUN | K. | ___ Park |
| U -12. HERSEY | L. | People suffered from ___ sickness & burns. |
| X -13. NAKAMURA | M. | River near Asano Park |
| P -14. SASAKI | N. | The bombs caused these & winds blew them out of control. |
| O -15. BOMBS | O. | Two were dropped on Japan. |
| T -16. TANIMOTO | P. | Doctor at Red Cross hospital; became wealthy |
| H -17. HAIR | Q. | City on which 2nd bomb was dropped |
| W -18. RIVERS | R. | Explosion-affected persons |
| B -19. JAPAN | S. | They dropped the bombs. |
| J -20. CLERK | T. | Pastor of Hiroshima Methodist Church |
| R -21. HIBAKUSHA | U. | Author |
| K -22. ASANO | V. | People drank contaminated ___. |
| F -23. PASTOR | W. | Waterways of Hiroshima |
| C -24. MR | X. | Tailor's widow with small children |
| V -25. WATER | Y. | Mrs. Nakamura's ___ machine rusted in her well. |

Copyrighted

Hiroshima Matching 4

___ 1. NAKAMURA        A. Staple food
___ 2. PASTOR          B. Doctor at Red Cross hospital; became wealthy
___ 3. SASAKI          C. Two were dropped on Japan.
___ 4. FIRES           D. Sasaki built these.
___ 5. LEUKEMIA        E. The bombs caused these & winds blew them out of control.
___ 6. SASKI           F. Fujii's occupation
___ 7. TANIMOTO        G. Kind of cloud in Hiroshima after the bomb
___ 8. BOMBS           H. Warning sound telling people to go to safe areas
___ 9. JAPAN           I. City on which 1st bomb was dropped
___10. SPAS            J. Waterways of Hiroshima
___11. KLEINSORGE      K. Explosion-affected persons
___12. HIROSHIMA       L. Country in which Hiroshima is located
___13. FUJII           M. German priest
___14. LIGHT           N. Saski eventually became one
___15. SLIGHTLY        O. Tanimoto's occupation
___16. DUST            P. One symptom of radiation sickness: ___ falls out
___17. SIREN           Q. East Parade Ground doctor's first duty was to take care of the ___ wounded
___18. RADIATION       R. People suffered from ___ sickness & burns.
___19. DOCTOR          S. Tailor's widow with small children
___20. RICE            T. Kind of bombs dropped on Japan
___21. NUN             U. People saw a bright ___ when the bomb went off.
___22. ATOMIC          V. Blood disease common among survivors
___23. HIBAKUSHA       W. Clerk at East Asia Tin Works trapped under bookcases
___24. HAIR            X. Pastor of Hiroshima Methodist Church
___25. RIVERS          Y. Doctor who owned & operated a private hospital

Hiroshima Matching 4 Answer Key

| | | |
|---|---|---|
| S - 1. NAKAMURA | A. | Staple food |
| O - 2. PASTOR | B. | Doctor at Red Cross hospital; became wealthy |
| B - 3. SASAKI | C. | Two were dropped on Japan. |
| E - 4. FIRES | D. | Sasaki built these. |
| V - 5. LEUKEMIA | E. | The bombs caused these & winds blew them out of control. |
| W - 6. SASKI | F. | Fujii's occupation |
| X - 7. TANIMOTO | G. | Kind of cloud in Hiroshima after the bomb |
| C - 8. BOMBS | H. | Warning sound telling people to go to safe areas |
| L - 9. JAPAN | I. | City on which 1st bomb was dropped |
| D - 10. SPAS | J. | Waterways of Hiroshima |
| M - 11. KLEINSORGE | K. | Explosion-affected persons |
| I - 12. HIROSHIMA | L. | Country in which Hiroshima is located |
| Y - 13. FUJII | M. | German priest |
| U - 14. LIGHT | N. | Saski eventually became one |
| Q - 15. SLIGHTLY | O. | Tanimoto's occupation |
| G - 16. DUST | P. | One symptom of radiation sickness: ___ falls out |
| H - 17. SIREN | Q. | East Parade Ground doctor's first duty was to take care of the ___ wounded |
| R - 18. RADIATION | R. | People suffered from ___ sickness & burns. |
| F - 19. DOCTOR | S. | Tailor's widow with small children |
| A - 20. RICE | T. | Kind of bombs dropped on Japan |
| N - 21. NUN | U. | People saw a bright ___ when the bomb went off. |
| T - 22. ATOMIC | V. | Blood disease common among survivors |
| K - 23. HIBAKUSHA | W. | Clerk at East Asia Tin Works trapped under bookcases |
| P - 24. HAIR | X. | Pastor of Hiroshima Methodist Church |
| J - 25. RIVERS | Y. | Doctor who owned & operated a private hospital |

Hiroshima Magic Squares 1

Match the definition with the vocabulary word. Put your answers in the magic squares below. When your answers are correct, all columns and rows will add to the same number.

| | | | |
|---|---|---|---|
| A. FAN | E. JAPAN | I. DOCTOR | M. TANIMOTO |
| B. KYO | F. MR | J. BOMBS | N. FUJII |
| C. CLERK | G. RIVERS | K. WATER | O. FIRES |
| D. NUN | H. NAGASAKI | L. SEWING | P. LEUKEMIA |

1. The bombs caused these & winds blew them out of control.
2. Two were dropped on Japan.
3. City on which 2nd bomb was dropped
4. Shape of the city of Hiroshima
5. Saski eventually became one
6. Country in which Hiroshima is located
7. People drank contaminated ___.
8. Doctor who owned & operated a private hospital
9. Nickname for the B29 bombers: ___. B
10. Saski's occupation
11. Pastor of Hiroshima Methodist Church
12. Mrs. Nakamura's ___ machine rusted in her well.
13. Fujii's occupation
14. Blood disease common among survivors
15. River near Asano Park
16. Waterways of Hiroshima

| A= | B= | C= | D= |
|---|---|---|---|
| E= | F= | G= | H= |
| I= | J= | K= | L= |
| M= | N= | O= | P= |

Hiroshima Magic Squares 1 Answer Key

Match the definition with the vocabulary word. Put your answers in the magic squares below. When your answers are correct, all columns and rows will add to the same number.

A. FAN        E. JAPAN       I. DOCTOR     M. TANIMOTO
B. KYO        F. MR          J. BOMBS      N. FUJII
C. CLERK      G. RIVERS      K. WATER      O. FIRES
D. NUN        H. NAGASAKI    L. SEWING     P. LEUKEMIA

1. The bombs caused these & winds blew them out of control.
2. Two were dropped on Japan.
3. City on which 2nd bomb was dropped
4. Shape of the city of Hiroshima
5. Saski eventually became one
6. Country in which Hiroshima is located
7. People drank contaminated ___.
8. Doctor who owned & operated a private hospital
9. Nickname for the B29 bombers: ___. B
10. Saski's occupation
11. Pastor of Hiroshima Methodist Church
12. Mrs. Nakamura's ___ machine rusted in her well.
13. Fujii's occupation
14. Blood disease common among survivors
15. River near Asano Park
16. Waterways of Hiroshima

| A=4 | B=15 | C=10 | D=5 |
| E=6 | F=9 | G=16 | H=3 |
| I=13 | J=2 | K=7 | L=12 |
| M=11 | N=8 | O=1 | P=14 |

Hiroshima Magic Squares 2

Match the definition with the vocabulary word. Put your answers in the magic squares below. When your answers are correct, all columns and rows will add to the same number.

A. LEUKEMIA      E. SPAS         I. LIGHT         M. CLERK
B. MR            F. RADIATION    J. DOCTOR        N. NAGASAKI
C. ATOMIC        G. FIRES        K. TANIMOTO      O. HAIR
D. DUST          H. AMERICANS    L. JAPAN         P. HIBAKUSHA

1. They dropped the bombs.
2. Blood disease common among survivors
3. Nickname for the B29 bombers: ___. B
4. The bombs caused these & winds blew them out of control.
5. Fujii's occupation
6. One symptom of radiation sickness: ___ falls out
7. Explosion-affected persons
8. People saw a bright ___ when the bomb went off.
9. Pastor of Hiroshima Methodist Church
10. City on which 2nd bomb was dropped
11. Saski's occupation
12. Country in which Hiroshima is located
13. Sasaki built these.
14. Kind of cloud in Hiroshima after the bomb
15. Kind of bombs dropped on Japan
16. People suffered from ___ sickness & burns.

| A= | B= | C= | D= |
| E= | F= | G= | H= |
| I= | J= | K= | L= |
| M= | N= | O= | P= |

Hiroshima Magic Squares 2 Answer Key

Match the definition with the vocabulary word. Put your answers in the magic squares below. When your answers are correct, all columns and rows will add to the same number.

A. LEUKEMIA
B. MR
C. ATOMIC
D. DUST
E. SPAS
F. RADIATION
G. FIRES
H. AMERICANS
I. LIGHT
J. DOCTOR
K. TANIMOTO
L. JAPAN
M. CLERK
N. NAGASAKI
O. HAIR
P. HIBAKUSHA

1. They dropped the bombs.
2. Blood disease common among survivors
3. Nickname for the B29 bombers: ___ B
4. The bombs caused these & winds blew them out of control.
5. Fujii's occupation
6. One symptom of radiation sickness: ___ falls out
7. Explosion-affected persons
8. People saw a bright ___ when the bomb went off.
9. Pastor of Hiroshima Methodist Church
10. City on which 2nd bomb was dropped
11. Saski's occupation
12. Country in which Hiroshima is located
13. Sasaki built these.
14. Kind of cloud in Hiroshima after the bomb
15. Kind of bombs dropped on Japan
16. People suffered from ___ sickness & burns.

| A=2 | B=3 | C=15 | D=14 |
| --- | --- | --- | --- |
| E=13 | F=16 | G=4 | H=1 |
| I=8 | J=5 | K=9 | L=12 |
| M=11 | N=10 | O=6 | P=7 |

Hiroshima Magic Squares 3

Match the definition with the vocabulary word. Put your answers in the magic squares below. When your answers are correct, all columns and rows will add to the same number.

A. SEWING
B. JAPAN
C. CLERK
D. RIVERS
E. RADIATION
F. AMERICANS
G. TANIMOTO
H. KLEINSORGE
I. MR
J. NAKAMURA
K. BOMBS
L. DOCTOR
M. SPAS
N. HOSPITALS
O. HIROSHIMA
P. NUN

1. City on which 1st bomb was dropped
2. Waterways of Hiroshima
3. Tailor's widow with small children
4. People suffered from ___ sickness & burns.
5. Nickname for the B29 bombers: ___. B
6. They dropped the bombs.
7. Saski eventually became one
8. Saski's occupation
9. German priest
10. Two were dropped on Japan.
11. Mrs. Nakamura's ___ machine rusted in her well.
12. Short-staffed, over-crowded places after the bombing
13. Country in which Hiroshima is located
14. Sasaki built these.
15. Pastor of Hiroshima Methodist Church
16. Fujii's occupation

| A= | B= | C= | D= |
| E= | F= | G= | H= |
| I= | J= | K= | L= |
| M= | N= | O= | P= |

Hiroshima Magic Squares 3 Answer Key

Match the definition with the vocabulary word. Put your answers in the magic squares below. When your answers are correct, all columns and rows will add to the same number.

| | | | |
|---|---|---|---|
| A. SEWING | E. RADIATION | I. MR | M. SPAS |
| B. JAPAN | F. AMERICANS | J. NAKAMURA | N. HOSPITALS |
| C. CLERK | G. TANIMOTO | K. BOMBS | O. HIROSHIMA |
| D. RIVERS | H. KLEINSORGE | L. DOCTOR | P. NUN |

1. City on which 1st bomb was dropped
2. Waterways of Hiroshima
3. Tailor's widow with small children
4. People suffered from ___ sickness & burns.
5. Nickname for the B29 bombers: ___. B
6. They dropped the bombs.
7. Saski eventually became one
8. Saski's occupation
9. German priest
10. Two were dropped on Japan.
11. Mrs. Nakamura's ___ machine rusted in her well.
12. Short-staffed, over-crowded places after the bombing
13. Country in which Hiroshima is located
14. Sasaki built these.
15. Pastor of Hiroshima Methodist Church
16. Fujii's occupation

| | | | |
|---|---|---|---|
| A=11 | B=13 | C=8 | D=2 |
| E=4 | F=6 | G=15 | H=9 |
| I=5 | J=3 | K=10 | L=16 |
| M=14 | N=12 | O=1 | P=7 |

Hiroshima Magic Squares 4

Match the definition with the vocabulary word. Put your answers in the magic squares below. When your answers are correct, all columns and rows will add to the same number.

| | | | |
|---|---|---|---|
| A. SASKI | E. FIRES | I. EXPLOSION | M. SLIGHTLY |
| B. SEWING | F. BOMBS | J. PASTOR | N. KLEINSORGE |
| C. PARK | G. LIGHT | K. DUST | O. SASAKI |
| D. FAN | H. HOSPITALS | L. MR | P. NAGASAKI |

1. Doctor at Red Cross hospital; became wealthy
2. Shape of the city of Hiroshima
3. Tanimoto's occupation
4. The bombs caused these & winds blew them out of control.
5. There was no sound of an ___ when the bomb went off.
6. Two were dropped on Japan.
7. City on which 2nd bomb was dropped
8. Asano ___
9. Short-staffed, over-crowded places after the bombing
10. Kind of cloud in Hiroshima after the bomb
11. Clerk at East Asia Tin Works trapped under bookcases
12. German priest
13. Mrs. Nakamura's ___ machine rusted in her well.
14. East Parade Ground doctor's first duty was to take care of the ___ wounded
15. People saw a bright ___ when the bomb went off.
16. Nickname for the B29 bombers: ___. B

| A= | B= | C= | D= |
|---|---|---|---|
| E= | F= | G= | H= |
| I= | J= | K= | L= |
| M= | N= | O= | P= |

Hiroshima Magic Squares 4 Answer Key

Match the definition with the vocabulary word. Put your answers in the magic squares below. When your answers are correct, all columns and rows will add to the same number.

A. SASKI  
B. SEWING  
C. PARK  
D. FAN  
E. FIRES  
F. BOMBS  
G. LIGHT  
H. HOSPITALS  
I. EXPLOSION  
J. PASTOR  
K. DUST  
L. MR  
M. SLIGHTLY  
N. KLEINSORGE  
O. SASAKI  
P. NAGASAKI  

1. Doctor at Red Cross hospital; became wealthy
2. Shape of the city of Hiroshima
3. Tanimoto's occupation
4. The bombs caused these & winds blew them out of control.
5. There was no sound of an ___ when the bomb went off.
6. Two were dropped on Japan.
7. City on which 2nd bomb was dropped
8. Asano ___
9. Short-staffed, over-crowded places after the bombing
10. Kind of cloud in Hiroshima after the bomb
11. Clerk at East Asia Tin Works trapped under bookcases
12. German priest
13. Mrs. Nakamura's ___ machine rusted in her well.
14. East Parade Ground doctor's first duty was to take care of the ___ wounded
15. People saw a bright ___ when the bomb went off.
16. Nickname for the B29 bombers: ___. B

| A=11 | B=13 | C=8 | D=2 |
| E=4 | F=6 | G=15 | H=9 |
| I=5 | J=3 | K=10 | L=16 |
| M=14 | N=12 | O=1 | P=7 |

Hiroshima Word Search 1

```
N T A N I M O T O S P N B L O O D T
A M E R I C A N S C A S C R S Q J G
G S P J L H D P P P X I R S V V R X
A S I R E N C H A A M I H S O R I H
S P S K U A E J O O S G L C N Q V Y
A A L X K K X S T S Q T D L A H E S
K R I M E A P A F M P W O M S I R W
I K G R M M L S C C D I C R A B S K
D H H F I U O A M L M T T K F A M G
G Y T Z A R S K Q G E T O A P K H Q
P F L J L A I I P N G R R I L U T F
B U Y E G R O S N I E L K H S S Q N
X J Q L T H N G H W C S Q B U H H P
J I X B L W J W R E A Y M D X A G L
L I G H T F I R E S Z O Y K S N U N
R X B T Z X A L T M B F P A G D B S
H R Y D K L D N A W T N P X M T G Z
R I C E H A I R W Y E S R E H R V Q
```

Asano ___ (4)
Author (6)
Blood disease common among survivors (8)
City on which 1st bomb was dropped (9)
City on which 2nd bomb was dropped (8)
Clerk at East Asia Tin Works trapped under bookcases (5)
Country in which Hiroshima is located (5)
Doctor at Red Cross hospital; became wealthy (6)
Doctor who owned & operated a private hospital (5)
East Parade Ground doctor's first duty was to take care of the ___ wounded (8)
Explosion-affected persons (9)
Fujii's occupation (6)
German priest (10)
Kind of bombs dropped on Japan (6)
Kind of cloud in Hiroshima after the bomb (4)
Mrs. Nakamura's ___ machine rusted in her well. (6)
Nickname for the B29 bombers: ___. B (2)
One symptom of radiation sickness: ___ falls out (4)
Pastor of Hiroshima Methodist Church (8)

People drank contaminated ___. (5)
People saw a bright ___ when the bomb went off. (5)
River near Asano Park (3)
Sasaki built these. (4)
Saski eventually became one (3)
Saski's occupation (5)
Shape of the city of Hiroshima (3)
Short-staffed, over-crowded places after the bombing (9)
Staple food (4)
Tailor's widow with small children (8)
Tanimoto's occupation (6)
The bombs caused these & winds blew them out of control. (5)
There was no sound of an ___ when the bomb went off. (9)
These disorders are common in the second stages of radiation sickness. (5)
They dropped the bombs. (9)
Two were dropped on Japan. (5)
Warning sound telling people to go to safe areas (5)
Waterways of Hiroshima (6)
___ Park (5)

Hiroshima Word Search 1 Answer Key

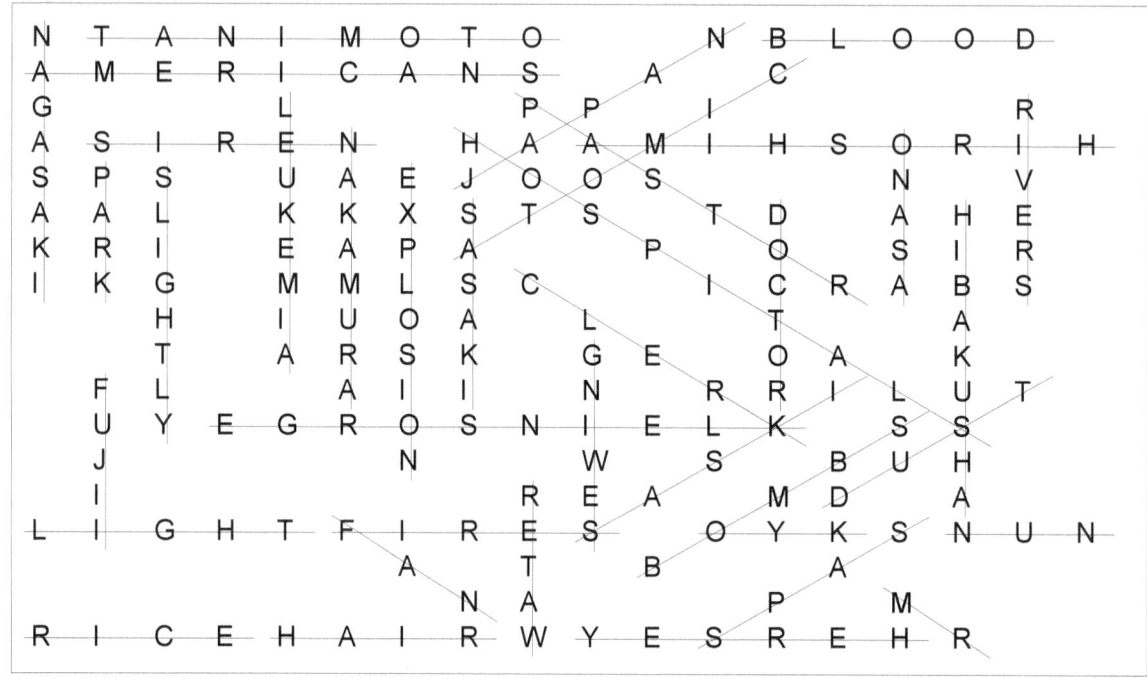

Asano ___ (4)
Author (6)
Blood disease common among survivors (8)
City on which 1st bomb was dropped (9)
City on which 2nd bomb was dropped (8)
Clerk at East Asia Tin Works trapped under bookcases (5)
Country in which Hiroshima is located (5)
Doctor at Red Cross hospital; became wealthy (6)
Doctor who owned & operated a private hospital (5)
East Parade Ground doctor's first duty was to take care of the ___ wounded (8)
Explosion-affected persons (9)
Fujii's occupation (6)
German priest (10)
Kind of bombs dropped on Japan (6)
Kind of cloud in Hiroshima after the bomb (4)
Mrs. Nakamura's ___ machine rusted in her well. (6)
Nickname for the B29 bombers: ___. B (2)
One symptom of radiation sickness: ___ falls out (4)
Pastor of Hiroshima Methodist Church (8)

People drank contaminated ___. (5)
People saw a bright ___ when the bomb went off. (5)
River near Asano Park (3)
Sasaki built these. (4)
Saski eventually became one (3)
Saski's occupation (5)
Shape of the city of Hiroshima (3)
Short-staffed, over-crowded places after the bombing (9)
Staple food (4)
Tailor's widow with small children (8)
Tanimoto's occupation (6)
The bombs caused these & winds blew them out of control. (5)
There was no sound of an ___ when the bomb went off. (9)
These disorders are common in the second stages of radiation sickness. (5)
They dropped the bombs. (9)
Two were dropped on Japan. (5)
Warning sound telling people to go to safe areas (5)
Waterways of Hiroshima (6)
___ Park (5)

Hiroshima Word Search 2

```
S I R E N J L W X P W Z Y D W B F Q
D E D N D Y V E S F A V K U J O I Q
N S W Z F X G C U A B R W S V M R K
Z P M I W A T E R K P C K T F B E X
S A X L N D B U J P E Y Y N J S S P
I S J H K G M Q O T O M I N A T B D
K L V I N A G J A M E R I C A N S M
A I R B K L X H D R V S Z A Q H W D
S G V A S J N O I S O L P X E E S B
A H N K K P O C T S J R F S R R H R
G T J U Z L J K H K D S I P I S Q M
A L W S B A C H G C Y G B V C E Z H
N Y P H P K L E I N S O R G E Y S Z
M U M A G W H M L Y F G O J G R A W
R T N K S W O F D H R N H S V H S R
C L E R K T R A D I A T I O N D K K
P X B G A N O N L S I I J U F B I J
S A S A K I V R A M W M R O T C O D
```

Asano ___ (4)
Author (6)
Blood disease common among survivors (8)
City on which 2nd bomb was dropped (8)
Clerk at East Asia Tin Works trapped under bookcases (5)
Country in which Hiroshima is located (5)
Doctor at Red Cross hospital; became wealthy (6)
Doctor who owned & operated a private hospital (5)
East Parade Ground doctor's first duty was to take care of the ___ wounded (8)
Explosion-affected persons (9)
Fujii's occupation (6)
German priest (10)
Kind of bombs dropped on Japan (6)
Kind of cloud in Hiroshima after the bomb (4)
Mrs. Nakamura's ___ machine rusted in her well. (6)
Nickname for the B29 bombers: ___. B (2)
One symptom of radiation sickness: ___ falls out (4)
Pastor of Hiroshima Methodist Church (8)
People drank contaminated ___. (5)

People saw a bright ___ when the bomb went off. (5)
People suffered from ___ sickness & burns. (9)
River near Asano Park (3)
Sasaki built these. (4)
Saski eventually became one (3)
Saski's occupation (5)
Shape of the city of Hiroshima (3)
Staple food (4)
Tailor's widow with small children (8)
Tanimoto's occupation (6)
The bombs caused these & winds blew them out of control. (5)
There was no sound of an ___ when the bomb went off. (9)
These disorders are common in the second stages of radiation sickness. (5)
They dropped the bombs. (9)
Two were dropped on Japan. (5)
Warning sound telling people to go to safe areas (5)
Waterways of Hiroshima (6)
___ Park (5)

Hiroshima Word Search 2 Answer Key

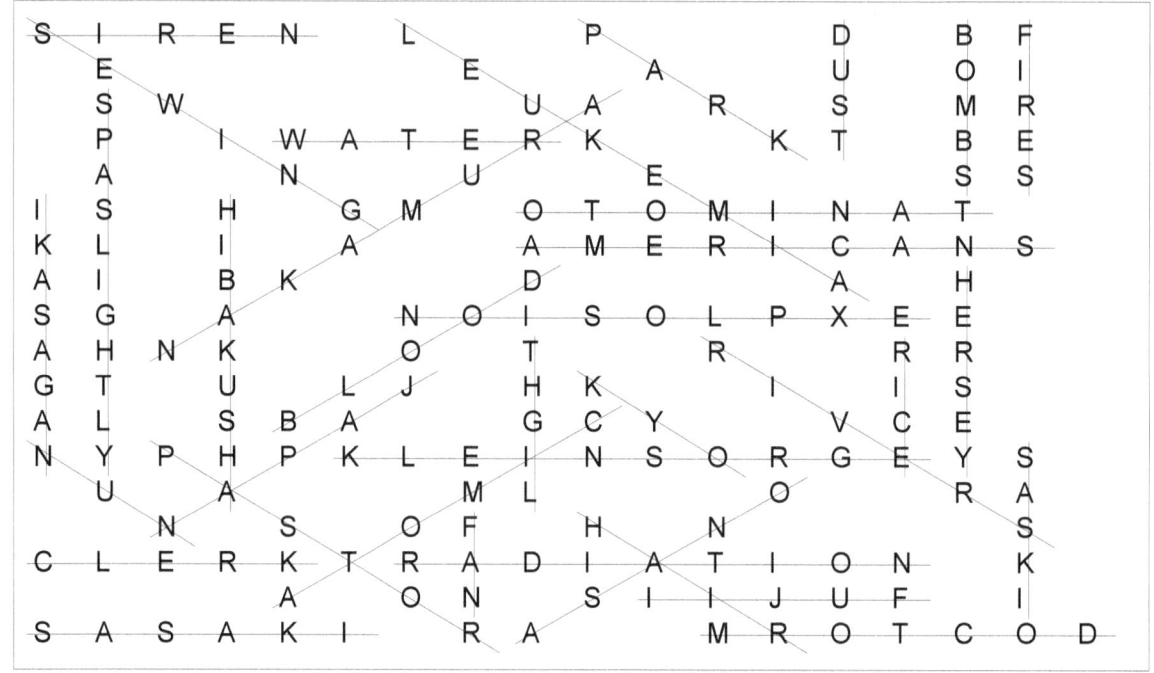

Asano ___ (4)
Author (6)
Blood disease common among survivors (8)
City on which 2nd bomb was dropped (8)
Clerk at East Asia Tin Works trapped under bookcases (5)
Country in which Hiroshima is located (5)
Doctor at Red Cross hospital; became wealthy (6)
Doctor who owned & operated a private hospital (5)
East Parade Ground doctor's first duty was to take care of the ___ wounded (8)
Explosion-affected persons (9)
Fujii's occupation (6)
German priest (10)
Kind of bombs dropped on Japan (6)
Kind of cloud in Hiroshima after the bomb (4)
Mrs. Nakamura's ___ machine rusted in her well. (6)
Nickname for the B29 bombers: ___. B (2)
One symptom of radiation sickness: ___ falls out (4)
Pastor of Hiroshima Methodist Church (8)
People drank contaminated ___. (5)

People saw a bright ___ when the bomb went off. (5)
People suffered from ___ sickness & burns. (9)
River near Asano Park (3)
Sasaki built these. (4)
Saski eventually became one (3)
Saski's occupation (5)
Shape of the city of Hiroshima (3)
Staple food (4)
Tailor's widow with small children (8)
Tanimoto's occupation (6)
The bombs caused these & winds blew them out of control. (5)
There was no sound of an ___ when the bomb went off. (9)
These disorders are common in the second stages of radiation sickness. (5)
They dropped the bombs. (9)
Two were dropped on Japan. (5)
Warning sound telling people to go to safe areas (5)
Waterways of Hiroshima (6)
___ Park (5)

## Hiroshima Word Search 3

```
E X P L O S I O N D G Q Y B L P S L A T
T A H G W P L B S P V Q I H L A K H T W
D M S S V K L E J J N K G S J S M T O Q
R E T H C P W V A S A K K K C T Y Z M D
R R A A Q I Y F P S L H L Y M O K K I W
S I R E N U N W A T E R E O K R E L C F
R C C G O I J S N N U N I R A I P B V C
T A F E I S M N K K K A N P S V F S C K
L N V M T N A O L K E K S D P E F K D L
J S K W A W N S T N M A O Z A R Y V J C
Z S T T I W V S K O I M R K S S Z D J J
L Z H P D C R N X I A U G P W W A O H K
B I R H A Z V L F Z T R E S Q H S O Y J
Y O G J R N W I Y R R A D U S T S L A X
T Q M H C C R J P O G M J U D P T B S N
L P F B T E M W T K K K Z I H V R A X
N C U K S W S C L P R A B T G L H M N X
F N J Y X B O C M N B Z A I Q C G Z O Q
L J I Z Y D G K R I P L L J D S V F H N
A M I H S O R I H F S S N A G A S A K I
```

| | | | |
|---|---|---|---|
| AMERICANS | FIRES | LEUKEMIA | RIVERS |
| ASANO | FUJII | LIGHT | SASAKI |
| ATOMIC | HAIR | MR | SASKI |
| BLOOD | HERSEY | NAGASAKI | SEWING |
| BOMBS | HIBAKUSHA | NAKAMURA | SIREN |
| CLERK | HIROSHIMA | NUN | SLIGHTLY |
| DOCTOR | HOSPITALS | PARK | SPAS |
| DUST | JAPAN | PASTOR | TANIMOTO |
| EXPLOSION | KLEINSORGE | RADIATION | WATER |
| FAN | KYO | RICE | |

# Hiroshima Word Search 3 Answer Key

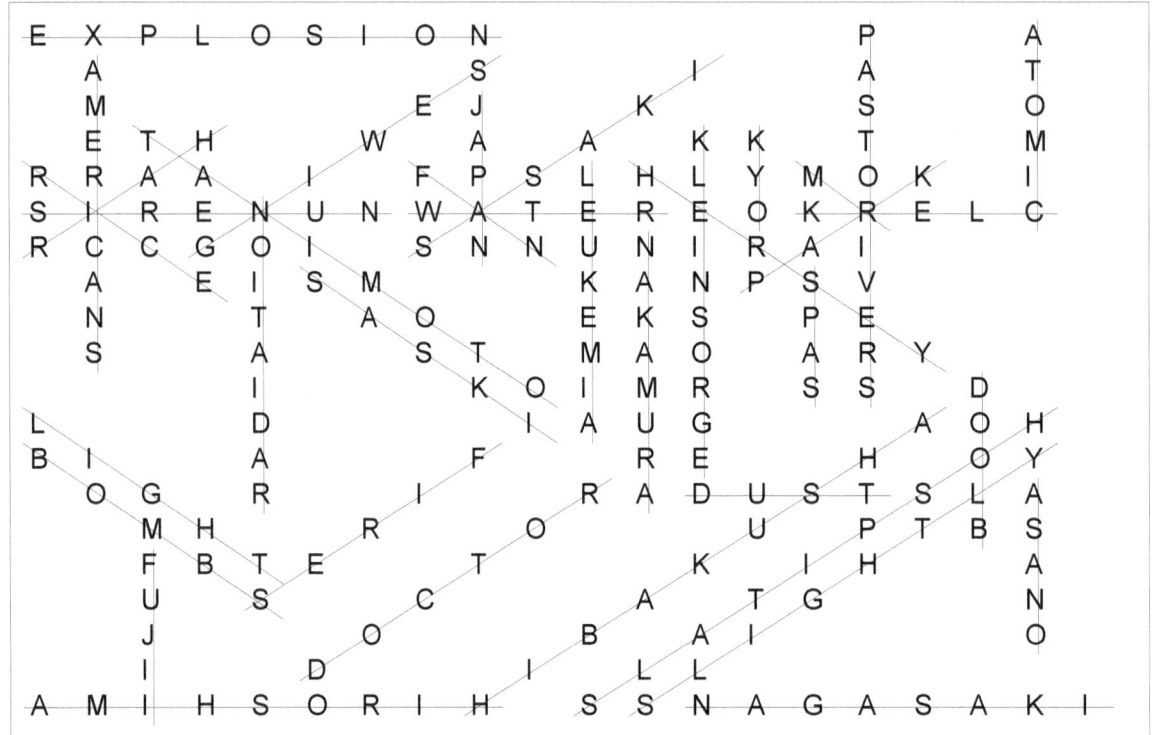

| AMERICANS | FIRES | LEUKEMIA | RIVERS |
| ASANO | FUJII | LIGHT | SASAKI |
| ATOMIC | HAIR | MR | SASKI |
| BLOOD | HERSEY | NAGASAKI | SEWING |
| BOMBS | HIBAKUSHA | NAKAMURA | SIREN |
| CLERK | HIROSHIMA | NUN | SLIGHTLY |
| DOCTOR | HOSPITALS | PARK | SPAS |
| DUST | JAPAN | PASTOR | TANIMOTO |
| EXPLOSION | KLEINSORGE | RADIATION | WATER |
| FAN | KYO | RICE | |

Hiroshima Word Search 4

```
M G B V T L N Z H F F M Y X W B N R L M
Z X J C F Q F B X W T Y D B K X S A M C
L S H H H P N T Y H F S Z C T J L D Y G
S L A G C P L T L X O T I L R O D I B P
M I S S L A S E S B Z S Q R T N O A H W
E G R P A R U G N W L J P O E U C T K R
X H I B A K U S H A T O M I C N T I M W
P T C X E S I A R H G I O M T S O O C J
L L E M C X I U C D N A G D U A R N L P
O Y I L Y R M M Q A S P S D T T L T E W
S A W A S A N O T R O T S A P H H S R H
I K D A K K G R L G Y C A V K G I C K N
O L V A T Z R I G N D W S H H I R K H V
N X N C S E R I F I T Y K L L L O W Y K
M T Q B R V R J V W J B I V Z G S F E O
J T M W H R Z U Y E D A G V T P H S S Q
D O K L N Q B F F S R B P F C H I H R G
B A M E R I C A N S W S M A J Y M L E X
X R N G X V P C S F Z S G N N Q A H H F
K L E I N S O R G E W G H B T Q Z V D C
```

| | | | |
|---|---|---|---|
| AMERICANS | FIRES | LEUKEMIA | RIVERS |
| ASANO | FUJII | LIGHT | SASAKI |
| ATOMIC | HAIR | MR | SASKI |
| BLOOD | HERSEY | NAGASAKI | SEWING |
| BOMBS | HIBAKUSHA | NAKAMURA | SIREN |
| CLERK | HIROSHIMA | NUN | SLIGHTLY |
| DOCTOR | HOSPITALS | PARK | SPAS |
| DUST | JAPAN | PASTOR | TANIMOTO |
| EXPLOSION | KLEINSORGE | RADIATION | WATER |
| FAN | KYO | RICE | |

# Hiroshima Word Search 4 Answer Key

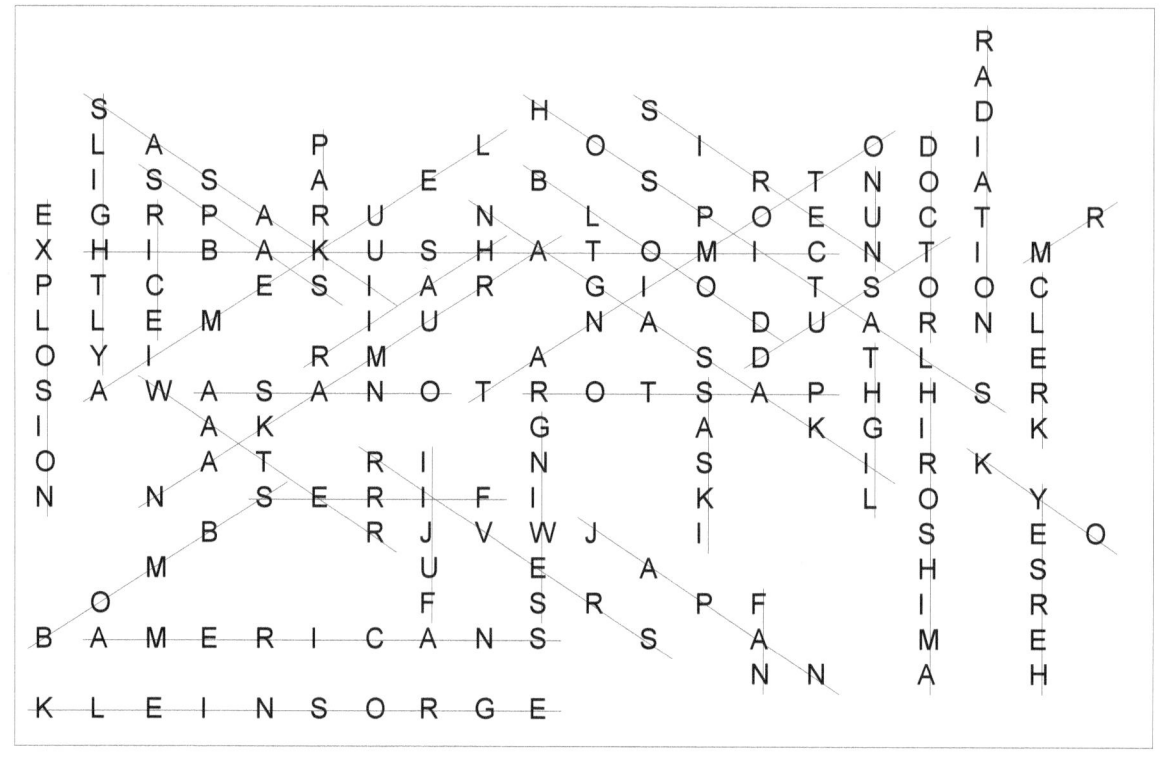

| AMERICANS | FIRES | LEUKEMIA | RIVERS |
| ASANO | FUJII | LIGHT | SASAKI |
| ATOMIC | HAIR | MR | SASKI |
| BLOOD | HERSEY | NAGASAKI | SEWING |
| BOMBS | HIBAKUSHA | NAKAMURA | SIREN |
| CLERK | HIROSHIMA | NUN | SLIGHTLY |
| DOCTOR | HOSPITALS | PARK | SPAS |
| DUST | JAPAN | PASTOR | TANIMOTO |
| EXPLOSION | KLEINSORGE | RADIATION | WATER |
| FAN | KYO | RICE | |

Hiroshima Crossword 1

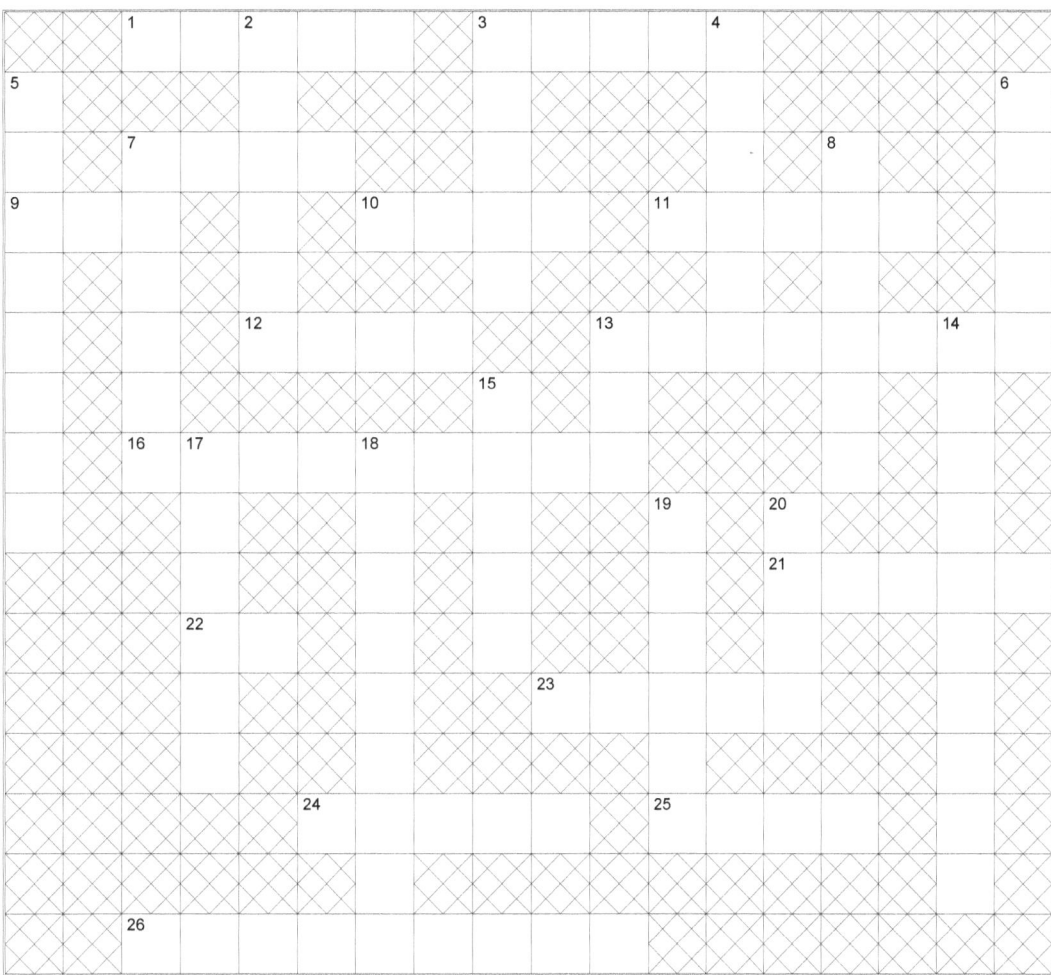

Across
1. Country in which Hiroshima is located
3. The bombs caused these & winds blew them out of control.
7. Kind of cloud in Hiroshima after the bomb
9. River near Asano Park
10. One symptom of radiation sickness: ___ falls out
11. Warning sound telling people to go to safe areas
12. Staple food
13. City on which 2nd bomb was dropped
16. People suffered from ___ sickness & burns.
21. ___ Park
22. Nickname for the B29 bombers: ___. B
23. Saski's occupation
24. People drank contaminated ___.
25. Sasaki built these.
26. City on which 1st bomb was dropped

Down
2. Tanimoto's occupation
3. Doctor who owned & operated a private hospital
4. Mrs. Nakamura's ___ machine rusted in her well.
5. Tailor's widow with small children
6. Clerk at East Asia Tin Works trapped under bookcases
7. Fujii's occupation
8. Author
13. Saski eventually became one
14. German priest
15. People saw a bright ___ when the bomb went off.
17. Kind of bombs dropped on Japan
18. They dropped the bombs.
19. Waterways of Hiroshima
20. Asano ___

Hiroshima Crossword 1 Answer Key

|   | 1 J | 2 P | A | N |   | 3 F | I | R | E | 4 S |   |   |   |
|---|---|---|---|---|---|---|---|---|---|---|---|---|---|
| 5 N |   |   | A |   |   | U |   |   |   | E |   |   | 6 S |
| A |   | 7 D | U | S | T |   | J |   |   | W |   | 8 H | A |
| 9 K | Y | O |   | T |   | 10 H | A | I | R | 11 S | I | R | E | N |   | S |
| A |   | C |   | O |   |   |   | I |   | N |   | R |   | K |
| M |   | T | 12 R | I | C | E |   | 13 N | A | G | A | S | 14 K | I |
| U |   | O |   |   | 15 L |   | U |   |   | E |   | L |   |
| R | 16 R | 17 A | D | I | 18 A | T | I | O | N |   |   | Y |   | E |
| A |   | T |   |   | M |   | G |   | 19 R | 20 P |   | I |   |
|   |   | O |   |   | E |   | H |   | I | 21 A | S | A | N | O |
|   | 22 M | R |   |   | R |   | T |   | V |   | R |   |   | S |
|   | I |   |   |   | I |   | 23 C | L | E | R | K |   |   | O |
|   | C |   |   |   | C |   |   |   | R |   |   |   |   | R |
|   | 24 W | A | T | E | R |   | 25 S | P | A | S |   |   | G |
|   |   |   |   | N |   |   |   |   |   |   |   |   | E |
|   | 26 H | I | R | O | S | H | I | M | A |   |   |   |   |

Across
1. Country in which Hiroshima is located
3. The bombs caused these & winds blew them out of control.
7. Kind of cloud in Hiroshima after the bomb
9. River near Asano Park
10. One symptom of radiation sickness: ___ falls out
11. Warning sound telling people to go to safe areas
12. Staple food
13. City on which 2nd bomb was dropped
16. People suffered from ___ sickness & burns.
21. ___ Park
22. Nickname for the B29 bombers: __. B
23. Saski's occupation
24. People drank contaminated ___.
25. Sasaki built these.
26. City on which 1st bomb was dropped

Down
2. Tanimoto's occupation
3. Doctor who owned & operated a private hospital
4. Mrs. Nakamura's ___ machine rusted in her well.
5. Tailor's widow with small children
6. Clerk at East Asia Tin Works trapped under bookcases
7. Fujii's occupation
8. Author
13. Saski eventually became one
14. German priest
15. People saw a bright ___ when the bomb went off.
17. Kind of bombs dropped on Japan
18. They dropped the bombs.
19. Waterways of Hiroshima
20. Asano ___

Hiroshima Crossword 2

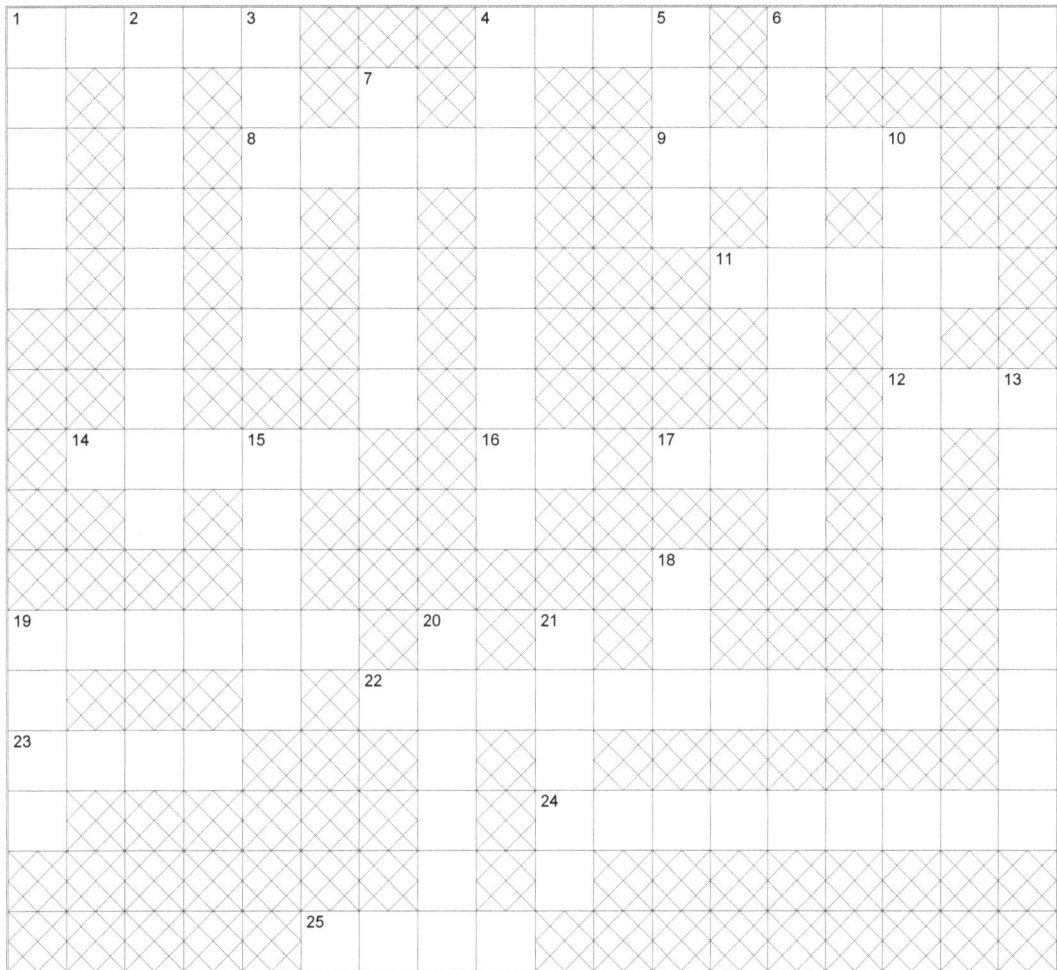

Across
1. The bombs caused these & winds blew them out of control.
4. One symptom of radiation sickness: ___ falls out
6. ___ Park
8. People drank contaminated ___.
9. Saski's occupation
11. Warning sound telling people to go to safe areas
12. Saski eventually became one
14. Two were dropped on Japan.
16. Nickname for the B29 bombers: ___. B
17. Shape of the city of Hiroshima
19. Fujii's occupation
22. Pastor of Hiroshima Methodist Church
23. Sasaki built these.
24. Explosion-affected persons
25. Asano ___

Down
1. Doctor who owned & operated a private hospital
2. People suffered from ___ sickness & burns.
3. Mrs. Nakamura's ___ machine rusted in her well.
4. City on which 1st bomb was dropped
5. Staple food
6. They dropped the bombs.
7. Kind of bombs dropped on Japan
10. German priest
13. Tailor's widow with small children
15. These disorders are common in the second stages of radiation sickness.
18. River near Asano Park
19. Kind of cloud in Hiroshima after the bomb
20. Tanimoto's occupation
21. People saw a bright ___ when the bomb went off.

Hiroshima Crossword 2 Answer Key

|   | 1 F | 2 I | 3 R | E | S |   |   | 4 H | A | I | R |   | 5 R |   | 6 A | S | A | N | O |
|---|---|---|---|---|---|---|---|---|---|---|---|---|---|---|---|---|---|---|---|
|   | U |   | A |   | E |   | 7 A |   | I |   |   |   | I |   | M |   |   |   |   |
|   | J |   | D |   | 8 W | A | T | E | R |   |   | 9 C | L | E | R | 10 K |   |   |   |
|   | I |   | I |   | I |   | O |   | O |   |   | E |   | R |   | L |   |   |   |
|   | I |   | A |   | N |   | M |   | S |   | 11 S | I | R | E | N |   |   |   |   |
|   |   |   | T |   | G |   | I |   | H |   |   |   |   | C |   | I |   |   |   |
|   |   |   | I |   |   |   | C |   | I |   |   |   |   | A |   | 12 N | 13 U | N |   |
|   |   | 14 B | O | M | 15 B | S |   | 16 M | R |   | 17 F | A | N |   | S |   | O | K | A |
|   |   |   | N |   | L |   |   | A |   |   |   | S |   | O |   | K |
|   |   |   |   |   | O |   |   | 18 K |   |   |   |   | R |   | A |
| 19 D | O | C | T | O | R |   | 20 P |   | 21 L | Y |   |   |   | G |   | M |
| U |   |   |   |   | 22 T | A | N | I | M | O | T | O |   | E |   | U |
| 23 S | P | A | S |   |   |   | I |   | S |   | G |   |   |   |   | R |
| T |   |   |   |   |   |   | 24 H | I | B | A | K | U | S | H | A |
|   |   |   |   |   |   |   | O |   | T |
|   |   |   |   | 25 P | A | R | K |

Across
1. The bombs caused these & winds blew them out of control.
4. One symptom of radiation sickness: ___ falls out
6. ___ Park
8. People drank contaminated ___.
9. Saski's occupation
11. Warning sound telling people to go to safe areas
12. Saski eventually became one
14. Two were dropped on Japan.
16. Nickname for the B29 bombers: ___. B
17. Shape of the city of Hiroshima
19. Fujii's occupation
22. Pastor of Hiroshima Methodist Church
23. Sasaki built these.
24. Explosion-affected persons
25. Asano ___

Down
1. Doctor who owned & operated a private hospital
2. People suffered from ___ sickness & burns.
3. Mrs. Nakamura's ___ machine rusted in her well.
4. City on which 1st bomb was dropped
5. Staple food
6. They dropped the bombs.
7. Kind of bombs dropped on Japan
10. German priest
13. Tailor's widow with small children
15. These disorders are common in the second stages of radiation sickness.
18. River near Asano Park
19. Kind of cloud in Hiroshima after the bomb
20. Tanimoto's occupation
21. People saw a bright ___ when the bomb went off.

Hiroshima Crossword 3

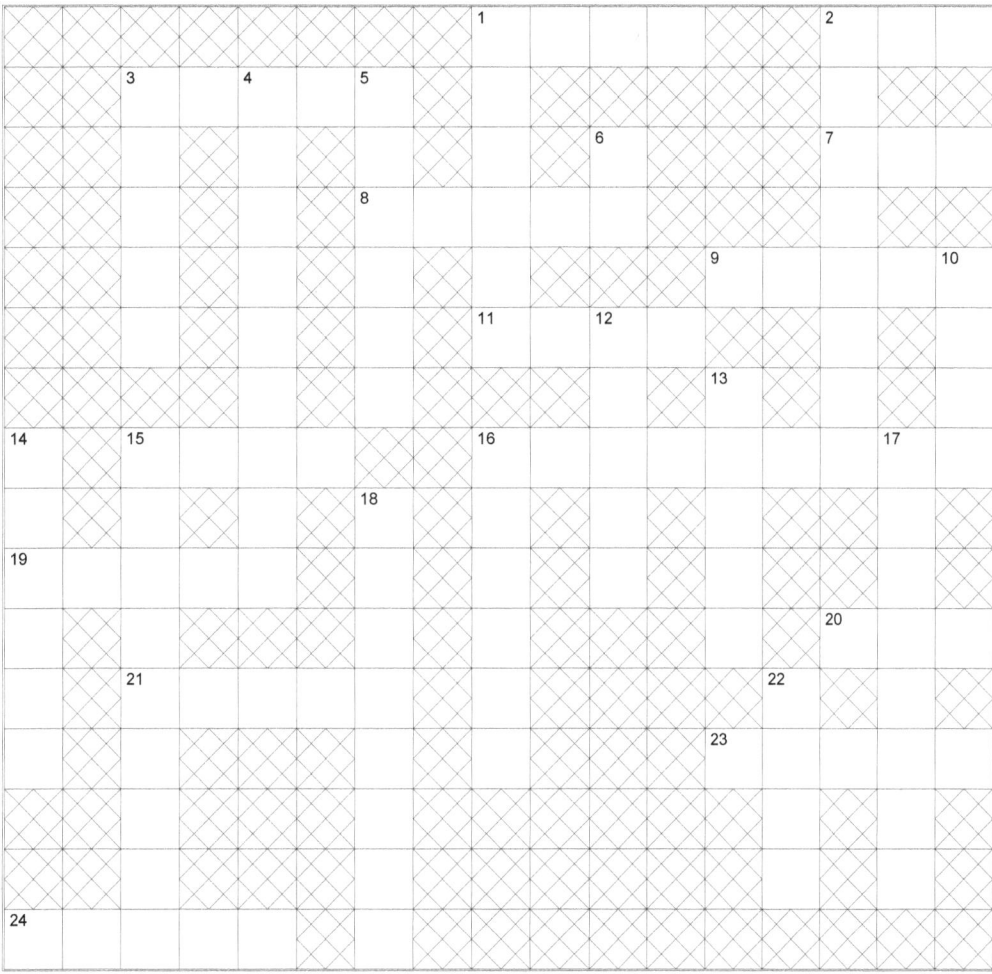

Across
1. Kind of cloud in Hiroshima after the bomb
2. Saski eventually became one
3. The bombs caused these & winds blew them out of control.
7. River near Asano Park
8. People drank contaminated ___.
9. Two were dropped on Japan.
11. Staple food
15. One symptom of radiation sickness: ___ falls out
16. They dropped the bombs.
19. Warning sound telling people to go to safe areas
20. Shape of the city of Hiroshima
21. Clerk at East Asia Tin Works trapped under bookcases
23. Country in which Hiroshima is located
24. ___ Park

Down
1. Fujii's occupation
2. Tailor's widow with small children
3. Doctor who owned & operated a private hospital
4. People suffered from ___ sickness & burns.
5. Mrs. Nakamura's ___ machine rusted in her well.
6. Nickname for the B29 bombers: ___. B
10. Sasaki built these.
12. Saski's occupation
13. People saw a bright ___ when the bomb went off.
14. Tanimoto's occupation
15. City on which 1st bomb was dropped
16. Kind of bombs dropped on Japan
17. City on which 2nd bomb was dropped
18. Pastor of Hiroshima Methodist Church
22. Asano ___

Hiroshima Crossword 3 Answer Key

|   |   |   |   |   |   | 1 D | U | S | T |   | 2 N | U | N |
|---|---|---|---|---|---|---|---|---|---|---|---|---|---|
|   | 3 F | 4 I | R | E | 5 S |   | O |   |   |   | A |   |   |
|   | U |   | A |   | E |   | C |   | 6 M |   | 7 K | Y | O |
|   | J |   | D |   | 8 W | A | T | E | R |   | A |   |   |
|   | I |   | I |   | I |   | O |   |   | 9 B | O | M | 10 B S |
|   | I |   | A |   | N |   | 11 R | 12 C | E |   | U |   | P |
|   |   |   | T |   | G |   |   | L |   | 13 L |   | R |   | A |
| 14 P |   | 15 H | A | I | R |   | 16 A | M | E | R | I | C | A | N 17 S |
| A |   | I |   |   |   | 18 T | T |   | R |   | G |   |   | A |
| 19 S | I | R | E | N |   | A |   | O |   | K |   | H |   |   | 20 F A N |
| T |   | O |   |   |   | N |   | M |   |   |   | T | 20 F | A | N |
| O |   | 21 S | A | S | K | I |   | I |   |   | 22 P |   | S |
| R |   | H |   |   | M |   | C |   |   | 23 J | A | P | A | N |
|   |   | I |   |   | O |   |   |   | R |   | K |   |   |
|   |   | M |   |   | T |   |   |   |   | K |   | I |   |
| 24 A | S | A | N | O |   | O |   |   |   |   |   |   |

**Across**
1. Kind of cloud in Hiroshima after the bomb
2. Saski eventually became one
3. The bombs caused these & winds blew them out of control.
7. River near Asano Park
8. People drank contaminated ___.
9. Two were dropped on Japan.
11. Staple food
15. One symptom of radiation sickness: ___ falls out
16. They dropped the bombs.
19. Warning sound telling people to go to safe areas
20. Shape of the city of Hiroshima
21. Clerk at East Asia Tin Works trapped under bookcases
23. Country in which Hiroshima is located
24. ___ Park

**Down**
1. Fujii's occupation
2. Tailor's widow with small children
3. Doctor who owned & operated a private hospital
4. People suffered from ___ sickness & burns.
5. Mrs. Nakamura's ___ machine rusted in her well.
6. Nickname for the B29 bombers: ___. B
10. Sasaki built these.
12. Saski's occupation
13. People saw a bright ___ when the bomb went off.
14. Tanimoto's occupation
15. City on which 1st bomb was dropped
16. Kind of bombs dropped on Japan
17. City on which 2nd bomb was dropped
18. Pastor of Hiroshima Methodist Church
22. Asano ___

Hiroshima Crossword 4

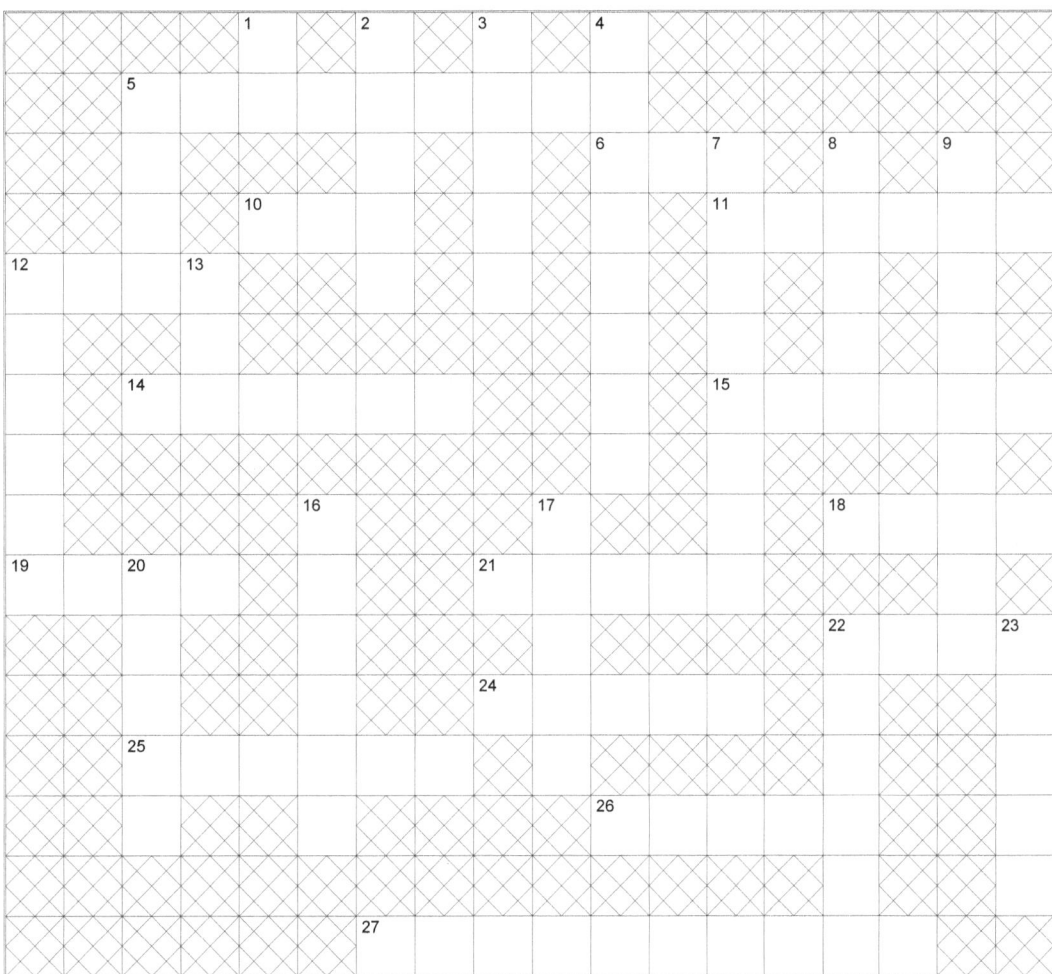

Across
5. City on which 1st bomb was dropped
6. Saski eventually became one
10. Shape of the city of Hiroshima
11. Kind of bombs dropped on Japan
12. Asano ___
14. Fujii's occupation
15. Doctor at Red Cross hospital; became wealthy
18. Kind of cloud in Hiroshima after the bomb
19. Staple food
21. Clerk at East Asia Tin Works trapped under bookcases
22. Sasaki built these.
24. People drank contaminated ___.
25. Waterways of Hiroshima
26. Doctor who owned & operated a private hospital
27. German priest

Down
1. Nickname for the B29 bombers: ___. B
2. ___ Park
3. People saw a bright ___ when the bomb went off.
4. Pastor of Hiroshima Methodist Church
5. One symptom of radiation sickness: ___ falls out
7. City on which 2nd bomb was dropped
8. Two were dropped on Japan.
9. Explosion-affected persons
12. Tanimoto's occupation
13. River near Asano Park
16. Author
17. Country in which Hiroshima is located
20. Saski's occupation
22. Mrs. Nakamura's ___ machine rusted in her well.
23. Warning sound telling people to go to safe areas

Hiroshima Crossword 4 Answer Key

|   |   |   |   | ¹M | ²A |   | ³L |   | ⁴T |   |   |   |
|---|---|---|---|---|---|---|---|---|---|---|---|---|
|   | ⁵H | I | R | O | S | H | I | M | A |   |   |   |
|   | A |   |   | S |   | G | ⁶N | U | ⁷N | ⁸B |   | ⁹H |
|   | I |   | ¹⁰F | A | N |   | I |   | ¹¹A | T | O | M | I | C |
| ¹²P | A | ¹³R | K |   | O |   | T |   | M | G |   | M | B |
| A |   | Y |   |   |   |   |   |   | O | A |   | B | A |
| S |   | ¹⁴D | O | C | T | O | R |   | T | ¹⁵S | A | S | A | K | I |
| T |   |   |   |   |   |   |   |   | O | A |   |   | U |
| O |   |   | ¹⁶H |   | ¹⁷J |   | K | ¹⁸D | U | S | T |
| ¹⁹R | ²⁰I | C | E |   | ²¹S | A | S | K | I |   |   | H |
|   | L |   | R |   | P |   |   |   | ²²S | P | A | ²³S |
|   | E |   | S |   | ²⁴W | A | T | E | R |   | E |   | I |
|   | ²⁵R | I | V | E | R | S |   | N |   |   | W |   | R |
|   | K |   | Y |   |   |   | ²⁶F | U | J | I | I |   | E |
|   |   |   |   |   |   |   |   |   |   |   | N |   | N |
|   |   |   |   | ²⁷K | L | E | I | N | S | O | R | G | E |

Across
5. City on which 1st bomb was dropped
6. Saski eventually became one
10. Shape of the city of Hiroshima
11. Kind of bombs dropped on Japan
12. Asano ___
14. Fujii's occupation
15. Doctor at Red Cross hospital; became wealthy
18. Kind of cloud in Hiroshima after the bomb
19. Staple food
21. Clerk at East Asia Tin Works trapped under bookcases
22. Sasaki built these.
24. People drank contaminated ___.
25. Waterways of Hiroshima
26. Doctor who owned & operated a private hospital
27. German priest

Down
1. Nickname for the B29 bombers: ___. B
2. ___ Park
3. People saw a bright ___ when the bomb went off.
4. Pastor of Hiroshima Methodist Church
5. One symptom of radiation sickness: ___ falls out
7. City on which 2nd bomb was dropped
8. Two were dropped on Japan.
9. Explosion-affected persons
12. Tanimoto's occupation
13. River near Asano Park
16. Author
17. Country in which Hiroshima is located
20. Saski's occupation
22. Mrs. Nakamura's ___ machine rusted in her well.
23. Warning sound telling people to go to safe areas

Hiroshima

| HIBAKUSHA | HERSEY | HOSPITALS | SPAS | PASTOR |
|---|---|---|---|---|
| ATOMIC | LIGHT | LEUKEMIA | RIVERS | NUN |
| NAGASAKI | SLIGHTLY | FREE SPACE | AMERICANS | DOCTOR |
| SEWING | SIREN | ASANO | FIRES | WATER |
| RADIATION | HAIR | EXPLOSION | KLEINSORGE | BLOOD |

Hiroshima

| RICE | FAN | JAPAN | SASAKI | KYO |
|---|---|---|---|---|
| TANIMOTO | BOMBS | DUST | HIROSHIMA | FUJII |
| CLERK | PARK | FREE SPACE | NAKAMURA | BLOOD |
| KLEINSORGE | EXPLOSION | HAIR | RADIATION | WATER |
| FIRES | ASANO | SIREN | SEWING | DOCTOR |

Hiroshima

| HERSEY | NUN | HOSPITALS | SASAKI | SLIGHTLY |
|---|---|---|---|---|
| DUST | JAPAN | DOCTOR | PARK | FAN |
| RICE | KYO | FREE SPACE | PASTOR | BOMBS |
| FIRES | HIBAKUSHA | LEUKEMIA | TANIMOTO | NAGASAKI |
| AMERICANS | SPAS | SASKI | SIREN | NAKAMURA |

Hiroshima

| WATER | HAIR | FUJII | LIGHT | ATOMIC |
|---|---|---|---|---|
| ASANO | RIVERS | KLEINSORGE | EXPLOSION | SEWING |
| HIROSHIMA | CLERK | FREE SPACE | BLOOD | NAKAMURA |
| SIREN | SASKI | SPAS | AMERICANS | NAGASAKI |
| TANIMOTO | LEUKEMIA | HIBAKUSHA | FIRES | BOMBS |

Hiroshima

| NAGASAKI | SIREN | SASKI | BLOOD | MR |
| --- | --- | --- | --- | --- |
| HERSEY | HOSPITALS | HIBAKUSHA | FUJII | SEWING |
| WATER | PARK | FREE SPACE | ATOMIC | RIVERS |
| BOMBS | SPAS | FAN | SASAKI | LEUKEMIA |
| DUST | JAPAN | FIRES | SLIGHTLY | HAIR |

Hiroshima

| NUN | LIGHT | TANIMOTO | ASANO | PASTOR |
| --- | --- | --- | --- | --- |
| AMERICANS | RADIATION | DOCTOR | NAKAMURA | CLERK |
| KYO | RICE | FREE SPACE | EXPLOSION | HAIR |
| SLIGHTLY | FIRES | JAPAN | DUST | LEUKEMIA |
| SASAKI | FAN | SPAS | BOMBS | RIVERS |

Hiroshima

| NUN | HAIR | PARK | MR | CLERK |
|---|---|---|---|---|
| PASTOR | SASKI | FIRES | DOCTOR | ATOMIC |
| RADIATION | JAPAN | FREE SPACE | RIVERS | BOMBS |
| TANIMOTO | NAGASAKI | RICE | FUJII | LEUKEMIA |
| HIROSHIMA | ASANO | HERSEY | SEWING | EXPLOSION |

Hiroshima

| KLEINSORGE | WATER | FAN | BLOOD | SLIGHTLY |
|---|---|---|---|---|
| SIREN | HIBAKUSHA | AMERICANS | SPAS | LIGHT |
| KYO | NAKAMURA | FREE SPACE | HOSPITALS | EXPLOSION |
| SEWING | HERSEY | ASANO | HIROSHIMA | LEUKEMIA |
| FUJII | RICE | NAGASAKI | TANIMOTO | BOMBS |

Hiroshima

| FAN | HIROSHIMA | LIGHT | EXPLOSION | KYO |
|---|---|---|---|---|
| SPAS | HAIR | FUJII | CLERK | NAKAMURA |
| ASANO | KLEINSORGE | FREE SPACE | SLIGHTLY | FIRES |
| DOCTOR | SEWING | WATER | RIVERS | NAGASAKI |
| SIREN | HOSPITALS | BOMBS | HERSEY | HIBAKUSHA |

Hiroshima

| SASAKI | NUN | PARK | MR | TANIMOTO |
|---|---|---|---|---|
| BLOOD | AMERICANS | PASTOR | RICE | DUST |
| ATOMIC | SASKI | FREE SPACE | JAPAN | HIBAKUSHA |
| HERSEY | BOMBS | HOSPITALS | SIREN | NAGASAKI |
| RIVERS | WATER | SEWING | DOCTOR | FIRES |

Hiroshima

| HIROSHIMA | NAKAMURA | KLEINSORGE | CLERK | BLOOD |
|---|---|---|---|---|
| PASTOR | AMERICANS | SASKI | SIREN | LIGHT |
| RADIATION | MR | FREE SPACE | RICE | HIBAKUSHA |
| BOMBS | HAIR | HOSPITALS | SPAS | EXPLOSION |
| JAPAN | DOCTOR | LEUKEMIA | WATER | SLIGHTLY |

Hiroshima

| PARK | TANIMOTO | FUJII | FIRES | NUN |
|---|---|---|---|---|
| KYO | ATOMIC | SASAKI | SEWING | NAGASAKI |
| ASANO | HERSEY | FREE SPACE | DUST | SLIGHTLY |
| WATER | LEUKEMIA | DOCTOR | JAPAN | EXPLOSION |
| SPAS | HOSPITALS | HAIR | BOMBS | HIBAKUSHA |

Hiroshima

| RIVERS | TANIMOTO | EXPLOSION | AMERICANS | SASAKI |
|---|---|---|---|---|
| HERSEY | DUST | KLEINSORGE | PASTOR | RICE |
| HAIR | JAPAN | FREE SPACE | ATOMIC | HIROSHIMA |
| BLOOD | CLERK | BOMBS | FAN | DOCTOR |
| LEUKEMIA | SLIGHTLY | NAGASAKI | HOSPITALS | WATER |

Hiroshima

| KYO | NUN | NAKAMURA | HIBAKUSHA | MR |
|---|---|---|---|---|
| SIREN | PARK | ASANO | SPAS | RADIATION |
| FUJII | FIRES | FREE SPACE | SASKI | WATER |
| HOSPITALS | NAGASAKI | SLIGHTLY | LEUKEMIA | DOCTOR |
| FAN | BOMBS | CLERK | BLOOD | HIROSHIMA |

Hiroshima

| ASANO | RIVERS | FIRES | TANIMOTO | SPAS |
|---|---|---|---|---|
| PARK | HIROSHIMA | DUST | RADIATION | WATER |
| NUN | AMERICANS | FREE SPACE | RICE | LIGHT |
| HAIR | SIREN | SLIGHTLY | EXPLOSION | SEWING |
| JAPAN | MR | BOMBS | FUJII | HERSEY |

Hiroshima

| DOCTOR | PASTOR | HOSPITALS | SASKI | FAN |
|---|---|---|---|---|
| KYO | KLEINSORGE | HIBAKUSHA | BLOOD | CLERK |
| NAKAMURA | LEUKEMIA | FREE SPACE | NAGASAKI | HERSEY |
| FUJII | BOMBS | MR | JAPAN | SEWING |
| EXPLOSION | SLIGHTLY | SIREN | HAIR | LIGHT |

Hiroshima

| NUN | AMERICANS | HAIR | ASANO | DOCTOR |
|---|---|---|---|---|
| RADIATION | PASTOR | FAN | KYO | KLEINSORGE |
| SLIGHTLY | HIROSHIMA | FREE SPACE | HIBAKUSHA | DUST |
| LEUKEMIA | HOSPITALS | BLOOD | MR | FIRES |
| ATOMIC | SEWING | RICE | PARK | SIREN |

Hiroshima

| SASKI | HERSEY | EXPLOSION | BOMBS | SASAKI |
|---|---|---|---|---|
| LIGHT | NAKAMURA | FUJII | RIVERS | JAPAN |
| SPAS | WATER | FREE SPACE | CLERK | SIREN |
| PARK | RICE | SEWING | ATOMIC | FIRES |
| MR | BLOOD | HOSPITALS | LEUKEMIA | DUST |

Hiroshima

| SEWING | RADIATION | SASKI | SASAKI | AMERICANS |
|---|---|---|---|---|
| RICE | DOCTOR | BOMBS | HERSEY | FIRES |
| FAN | HIROSHIMA | FREE SPACE | LEUKEMIA | ATOMIC |
| KLEINSORGE | HAIR | LIGHT | SPAS | NAGASAKI |
| SLIGHTLY | NAKAMURA | SIREN | EXPLOSION | DUST |

Hiroshima

| WATER | PASTOR | JAPAN | HOSPITALS | PARK |
|---|---|---|---|---|
| TANIMOTO | RIVERS | HIBAKUSHA | KYO | FUJII |
| NUN | ASANO | FREE SPACE | MR | DUST |
| EXPLOSION | SIREN | NAKAMURA | SLIGHTLY | NAGASAKI |
| SPAS | LIGHT | HAIR | KLEINSORGE | ATOMIC |

Hiroshima

| LIGHT | MR | SLIGHTLY | PASTOR | RADIATION |
|---|---|---|---|---|
| NAGASAKI | FAN | HERSEY | EXPLOSION | KLEINSORGE |
| SEWING | FUJII | FREE SPACE | DOCTOR | LEUKEMIA |
| HIROSHIMA | RICE | HIBAKUSHA | NUN | RIVERS |
| WATER | HAIR | TANIMOTO | DUST | SASAKI |

Hiroshima

| KYO | BOMBS | CLERK | HOSPITALS | ATOMIC |
|---|---|---|---|---|
| BLOOD | AMERICANS | FIRES | JAPAN | SPAS |
| SIREN | NAKAMURA | FREE SPACE | PARK | SASAKI |
| DUST | TANIMOTO | HAIR | WATER | RIVERS |
| NUN | HIBAKUSHA | RICE | HIROSHIMA | LEUKEMIA |

Hiroshima

| CLERK | LEUKEMIA | ASANO | ATOMIC | MR |
|---|---|---|---|---|
| PARK | WATER | HERSEY | DUST | RIVERS |
| BLOOD | NAGASAKI | FREE SPACE | KLEINSORGE | BOMBS |
| EXPLOSION | SIREN | FAN | SASKI | PASTOR |
| DOCTOR | HIROSHIMA | SLIGHTLY | SPAS | FIRES |

Hiroshima

| LIGHT | FUJII | HOSPITALS | SASAKI | RICE |
|---|---|---|---|---|
| HAIR | NAKAMURA | HIBAKUSHA | TANIMOTO | SEWING |
| AMERICANS | RADIATION | FREE SPACE | JAPAN | FIRES |
| SPAS | SLIGHTLY | HIROSHIMA | DOCTOR | PASTOR |
| SASKI | FAN | SIREN | EXPLOSION | BOMBS |

Hiroshima

| HIROSHIMA | FIRES | HOSPITALS | SLIGHTLY | SASAKI |
|---|---|---|---|---|
| HIBAKUSHA | HERSEY | RICE | BOMBS | LEUKEMIA |
| LIGHT | NAKAMURA | FREE SPACE | SEWING | MR |
| CLERK | BLOOD | RADIATION | TANIMOTO | SASKI |
| ASANO | WATER | KYO | NAGASAKI | FAN |

Hiroshima

| HAIR | NUN | SPAS | AMERICANS | PARK |
|---|---|---|---|---|
| PASTOR | EXPLOSION | FUJII | RIVERS | JAPAN |
| ATOMIC | DUST | FREE SPACE | SIREN | FAN |
| NAGASAKI | KYO | WATER | ASANO | SASKI |
| TANIMOTO | RADIATION | BLOOD | CLERK | MR |

Hiroshima

| SPAS | HOSPITALS | DUST | RADIATION | JAPAN |
|---|---|---|---|---|
| FAN | FIRES | SLIGHTLY | KYO | WATER |
| DOCTOR | SASAKI | FREE SPACE | BLOOD | FUJII |
| RIVERS | SIREN | ASANO | LEUKEMIA | PARK |
| NUN | NAGASAKI | KLEINSORGE | ATOMIC | EXPLOSION |

Hiroshima

| HIROSHIMA | HERSEY | HAIR | SASKI | LIGHT |
|---|---|---|---|---|
| PASTOR | NAKAMURA | RICE | TANIMOTO | BOMBS |
| SEWING | CLERK | FREE SPACE | AMERICANS | EXPLOSION |
| ATOMIC | KLEINSORGE | NAGASAKI | NUN | PARK |
| LEUKEMIA | ASANO | SIREN | RIVERS | FUJII |

Hiroshima

| NUN | SLIGHTLY | ASANO | KLEINSORGE | HERSEY |
|---|---|---|---|---|
| LIGHT | DUST | HOSPITALS | RIVERS | CLERK |
| NAGASAKI | JAPAN | FREE SPACE | SEWING | KYO |
| TANIMOTO | NAKAMURA | SIREN | HAIR | HIROSHIMA |
| AMERICANS | SASAKI | FAN | SPAS | BOMBS |

Hiroshima

| LEUKEMIA | MR | RADIATION | PASTOR | BLOOD |
|---|---|---|---|---|
| ATOMIC | SASKI | RICE | FUJII | DOCTOR |
| EXPLOSION | WATER | FREE SPACE | HIBAKUSHA | BOMBS |
| SPAS | FAN | SASAKI | AMERICANS | HIROSHIMA |
| HAIR | SIREN | NAKAMURA | TANIMOTO | KYO |

Hiroshima

| SASAKI | AMERICANS | NAGASAKI | SEWING | HAIR |
|---|---|---|---|---|
| HOSPITALS | HERSEY | FIRES | EXPLOSION | MR |
| FUJII | KLEINSORGE | FREE SPACE | SIREN | PASTOR |
| WATER | NAKAMURA | BOMBS | ASANO | JAPAN |
| LIGHT | RICE | HIROSHIMA | SASKI | SPAS |

Hiroshima

| DUST | LEUKEMIA | SLIGHTLY | DOCTOR | NUN |
|---|---|---|---|---|
| TANIMOTO | CLERK | ATOMIC | RIVERS | RADIATION |
| KYO | PARK | FREE SPACE | FAN | SPAS |
| SASKI | HIROSHIMA | RICE | LIGHT | JAPAN |
| ASANO | BOMBS | NAKAMURA | WATER | PASTOR |

# Hiroshima Vocabulary Word List

| No. | Word | Clue/Definition |
|---|---|---|
| 1. | APATHETIC | Uncaring; uninterested |
| 2. | ATAVISTIC | Return of a trait after a period of absence |
| 3. | ATTITUDINIZING | Assuming a false attitude; posturing |
| 4. | BREVIARY | Book containing hymns and prayers |
| 5. | BUFFETED | Forced; battered |
| 6. | CAPRICIOUS | Unpredictable |
| 7. | CATECHIST | One who teaches Christian doctrines |
| 8. | CHAGRIN | Feeling of embarrassment or humiliation caused by failure or disappointment |
| 9. | CHARRED | Scorched |
| 10. | CONSECRATE | Make sacred |
| 11. | CONTUSIONS | Bruises |
| 12. | CONVIVIAL | Sociable |
| 13. | CRUX | Basic, central, or critical point |
| 14. | DECREPIT | Worn out; broken down from use |
| 15. | EFFACIOUS | Producing the desired effect |
| 16. | EMANATION | Something coming forth from a source |
| 17. | EXTRICATED | Pulled out |
| 18. | HEDONISTIC | Characterized by the pursuit of sensual pleasure |
| 19. | HEINOUS | Horrible; abominable; reprehensible |
| 20. | INCENDIARY | Of or containing chemicals that cause fire when exploded |
| 21. | INTERMITTENT | Stopping and starting at intervals |
| 22. | MALAISE | Sense of bodily discomfort, depression, or unease |
| 23. | MIASMA | Poisonous atmosphere |
| 24. | MORIBUND | About to die |
| 25. | OSTENSIBLY | Represented or appearing as such |
| 26. | PAROXYSM | Sudden outburst |
| 27. | POMMELED | Beat; hit |
| 28. | PRECARIOUS | Dangerously lacking in security or stability |
| 29. | PREFECTURAL | District administered or governed by a prefect |
| 30. | PUTRESCENCE | Decomposed, rotten, foul-smelling matter |
| 31. | RECONNAISSANCE | Exploration of an area to gather information |
| 32. | REPUGNANT | Repulsive; disgusting; offensive |
| 33. | RUDIMENTARY | Basic; at the roots |
| 34. | SOLICITOUS | Marked by anxious care and attentiveness |
| 35. | STUPEFIED | With senses dulled by amazement |
| 36. | SUCCINCT | Short and to the point |
| 37. | SUPPURATED | Full of pus |
| 38. | SYBARITES | People devoted to pleasure and luxury |
| 39. | TALISMANIC | Magical |
| 40. | VOLITION | Conscious decision |
| 41. | XENOPHOBIC | Having a fear of foreigners |
| 42. | YEN | Japanese money |

Hiroshima Vocabulary Fill In The Blanks 1

1. Make sacred
2. Worn out; broken down from use
3. About to die
4. Repulsive; disgusting; offensive
5. Uncaring; uninterested
6. Sociable
7. Characterized by the pursuit of sensual pleasure
8. Exploration of an area to gather information
9. Marked by anxious care and attentiveness
10. Dangerously lacking in security or stability
11. Of or containing chemicals that cause fire when exploded
12. People devoted to pleasure and luxury
13. Short and to the point
14. Stopping and starting at intervals
15. Bruises
16. Decomposed, rotten, foul-smelling matter
17. Represented or appearing as such
18. Magical
19. Return of a trait after a period of absence
20. Poisonous atmosphere

Hiroshima Vocabulary Fill In The Blanks 1 Answer Key

| | |
|---|---|
| CONSECRATE | 1. Make sacred |
| DECREPIT | 2. Worn out; broken down from use |
| MORIBUND | 3. About to die |
| REPUGNANT | 4. Repulsive; disgusting; offensive |
| APATHETIC | 5. Uncaring; uninterested |
| CONVIVIAL | 6. Sociable |
| HEDONISTIC | 7. Characterized by the pursuit of sensual pleasure |
| RECONNAISSANCE | 8. Exploration of an area to gather information |
| SOLICITOUS | 9. Marked by anxious care and attentiveness |
| PRECARIOUS | 10. Dangerously lacking in security or stability |
| INCENDIARY | 11. Of or containing chemicals that cause fire when exploded |
| SYBARITES | 12. People devoted to pleasure and luxury |
| SUCCINCT | 13. Short and to the point |
| INTERMITTENT | 14. Stopping and starting at intervals |
| CONTUSIONS | 15. Bruises |
| PUTRESCENCE | 16. Decomposed, rotten, foul-smelling matter |
| OSTENSIBLY | 17. Represented or appearing as such |
| TALISMANIC | 18. Magical |
| ATAVISTIC | 19. Return of a trait after a period of absence |
| MIASMA | 20. Poisonous atmosphere |

Hiroshima Vocabulary Fill In The Blanks 2

1. Forced; battered
2. Assuming a false attitude; posturing
3. Bruises
4. Something coming forth from a source
5. Characterized by the pursuit of sensual pleasure
6. Unpredictable
7. Return of a trait after a period of absence
8. Basic; at the roots
9. Marked by anxious care and attentiveness
10. Sociable
11. Short and to the point
12. Book containing hymns and prayers
13. One who teaches Christian doctrines
14. Full of pus
15. Magical
16. Exploration of an area to gather information
17. Conscious decision
18. Stopping and starting at intervals
19. Pulled out
20. Basic, central, or critical point

Hiroshima Vocabulary Fill In The Blanks 2 Answer Key

|  |  |
|---|---|
| BUFFETED | 1. Forced; battered |
| ATTITUDINIZING | 2. Assuming a false attitude; posturing |
| CONTUSIONS | 3. Bruises |
| EMANATION | 4. Something coming forth from a source |
| HEDONISTIC | 5. Characterized by the pursuit of sensual pleasure |
| CAPRICIOUS | 6. Unpredictable |
| ATAVISTIC | 7. Return of a trait after a period of absence |
| RUDIMENTARY | 8. Basic; at the roots |
| SOLICITOUS | 9. Marked by anxious care and attentiveness |
| CONVIVIAL | 10. Sociable |
| SUCCINCT | 11. Short and to the point |
| BREVIARY | 12. Book containing hymns and prayers |
| CATECHIST | 13. One who teaches Christian doctrines |
| SUPPURATED | 14. Full of pus |
| TALISMANIC | 15. Magical |
| RECONNAISSANCE | 16. Exploration of an area to gather information |
| VOLITION | 17. Conscious decision |
| INTERMITTENT | 18. Stopping and starting at intervals |
| EXTRICATED | 19. Pulled out |
| CRUX | 20. Basic, central, or critical point |

Hiroshima Vocabulary Fill In The Blanks 3

1. Magical
2. With senses dulled by amazement
3. About to die
4. Sense of bodily discomfort, depression, or unease
5. Full of pus
6. Return of a trait after a period of absence
7. Basic; at the roots
8. Beat; hit
9. Sudden outburst
10. Scorched
11. Poisonous atmosphere
12. Something coming forth from a source
13. Uncaring; uninterested
14. Of or containing chemicals that cause fire when exploded
15. Decomposed, rotten, foul-smelling matter
16. Producing the desired effect
17. Exploration of an area to gather information
18. Make sacred
19. Characterized by the pursuit of sensual pleasure
20. District administered or governed by a prefect

Hiroshima Vocabulary Fill In The Blanks 3 Answer Key

| | |
|---|---|
| TALISMANIC | 1. Magical |
| STUPEFIED | 2. With senses dulled by amazement |
| MORIBUND | 3. About to die |
| MALAISE | 4. Sense of bodily discomfort, depression, or unease |
| SUPPURATED | 5. Full of pus |
| ATAVISTIC | 6. Return of a trait after a period of absence |
| RUDIMENTARY | 7. Basic; at the roots |
| POMMELED | 8. Beat; hit |
| PAROXYSM | 9. Sudden outburst |
| CHARRED | 10. Scorched |
| MIASMA | 11. Poisonous atmosphere |
| EMANATION | 12. Something coming forth from a source |
| APATHETIC | 13. Uncaring; uninterested |
| INCENDIARY | 14. Of or containing chemicals that cause fire when exploded |
| PUTRESCENCE | 15. Decomposed, rotten, foul-smelling matter |
| EFFACIOUS | 16. Producing the desired effect |
| RECONNAISSANCE | 17. Exploration of an area to gather information |
| CONSECRATE | 18. Make sacred |
| HEDONISTIC | 19. Characterized by the pursuit of sensual pleasure |
| PREFECTURAL | 20. District administered or governed by a prefect |

Hiroshima Vocabulary Fill In The Blanks 4

1. Decomposed, rotten, foul-smelling matter
2. Of or containing chemicals that cause fire when exploded
3. Short and to the point
4. Exploration of an area to gather information
5. Basic, central, or critical point
6. Producing the desired effect
7. Book containing hymns and prayers
8. Uncaring; uninterested
9. Assuming a false attitude; posturing
10. Conscious decision
11. District administered or governed by a prefect
12. Stopping and starting at intervals
13. Unpredictable
14. Scorched
15. Full of pus
16. Japanese money
17. Return of a trait after a period of absence
18. Horrible; abominable; reprehensible
19. Beat; hit
20. Having a fear of foreigners

Hiroshima Vocabulary Fill In The Blanks 4 Answer Key

| | |
|---|---|
| PUTRESCENCE | 1. Decomposed, rotten, foul-smelling matter |
| INCENDIARY | 2. Of or containing chemicals that cause fire when exploded |
| SUCCINCT | 3. Short and to the point |
| RECONNAISSANCE | 4. Exploration of an area to gather information |
| CRUX | 5. Basic, central, or critical point |
| EFFACIOUS | 6. Producing the desired effect |
| BREVIARY | 7. Book containing hymns and prayers |
| APATHETIC | 8. Uncaring; uninterested |
| ATTITUDINIZING | 9. Assuming a false attitude; posturing |
| VOLITION | 10. Conscious decision |
| PREFECTURAL | 11. District administered or governed by a prefect |
| INTERMITTENT | 12. Stopping and starting at intervals |
| CAPRICIOUS | 13. Unpredictable |
| CHARRED | 14. Scorched |
| SUPPURATED | 15. Full of pus |
| YEN | 16. Japanese money |
| ATAVISTIC | 17. Return of a trait after a period of absence |
| HEINOUS | 18. Horrible; abominable; reprehensible |
| POMMELED | 19. Beat; hit |
| XENOPHOBIC | 20. Having a fear of foreigners |

Hiroshima Vocabulary Matching 1

___ 1. EFFACIOUS          A. Something coming forth from a source
___ 2. VOLITION           B. Basic, central, or critical point
___ 3. HEDONISTIC         C. With senses dulled by amazement
___ 4. SYBARITES          D. Full of pus
___ 5. SUCCINCT           E. Sense of bodily discomfort, depression, or unease
___ 6. YEN                F. Assuming a false attitude; posturing
___ 7. CRUX               G. Feeling of embarrassment or humiliation caused by failure or disappointment
___ 8. RECONNAISSANCE     H. Of or containing chemicals that cause fire when exploded
___ 9. INCENDIARY         I. People devoted to pleasure and luxury
___10. MORIBUND           J. Characterized by the pursuit of sensual pleasure
___11. CAPRICIOUS         K. Short and to the point
___12. OSTENSIBLY         L. Conscious decision
___13. CATECHIST          M. Bruises
___14. CONTUSIONS         N. About to die
___15. ATTITUDINIZING     O. Japanese money
___16. SUPPURATED         P. Decomposed, rotten, foul-smelling matter
___17. INTERMITTENT       Q. Stopping and starting at intervals
___18. RUDIMENTARY        R. Unpredictable
___19. MALAISE            S. Represented or appearing as such
___20. DECREPIT           T. Exploration of an area to gather information
___21. EMANATION          U. Producing the desired effect
___22. ATAVISTIC          V. Return of a trait after a period of absence
___23. CHAGRIN            W. Worn out; broken down from use
___24. PUTRESCENCE        X. One who teaches Christian doctrines
___25. STUPEFIED          Y. Basic; at the roots

Hiroshima Vocabulary Matching 1 Answer Key

| | | |
|---|---|---|
| U - 1. EFFACIOUS | A. | Something coming forth from a source |
| L - 2. VOLITION | B. | Basic, central, or critical point |
| J - 3. HEDONISTIC | C. | With senses dulled by amazement |
| I - 4. SYBARITES | D. | Full of pus |
| K - 5. SUCCINCT | E. | Sense of bodily discomfort, depression, or unease |
| O - 6. YEN | F. | Assuming a false attitude; posturing |
| B - 7. CRUX | G. | Feeling of embarrassment or humiliation caused by failure or disappointment |
| T - 8. RECONNAISSANCE | H. | Of or containing chemicals that cause fire when exploded |
| H - 9. INCENDIARY | I. | People devoted to pleasure and luxury |
| N -10. MORIBUND | J. | Characterized by the pursuit of sensual pleasure |
| R -11. CAPRICIOUS | K. | Short and to the point |
| S -12. OSTENSIBLY | L. | Conscious decision |
| X -13. CATECHIST | M. | Bruises |
| M -14. CONTUSIONS | N. | About to die |
| F -15. ATTITUDINIZING | O. | Japanese money |
| D -16. SUPPURATED | P. | Decomposed, rotten, foul-smelling matter |
| Q -17. INTERMITTENT | Q. | Stopping and starting at intervals |
| Y -18. RUDIMENTARY | R. | Unpredictable |
| E -19. MALAISE | S. | Represented or appearing as such |
| W -20. DECREPIT | T. | Exploration of an area to gather information |
| A -21. EMANATION | U. | Producing the desired effect |
| V -22. ATAVISTIC | V. | Return of a trait after a period of absence |
| G -23. CHAGRIN | W. | Worn out; broken down from use |
| P -24. PUTRESCENCE | X. | One who teaches Christian doctrines |
| C -25. STUPEFIED | Y. | Basic; at the roots |

Hiroshima Vocabulary Matching 2

___ 1. MALAISE                A. Forced; battered
___ 2. CAPRICIOUS             B. Sense of bodily discomfort, depression, or unease
___ 3. PUTRESCENCE            C. Marked by anxious care and attentiveness
___ 4. APATHETIC              D. Magical
___ 5. TALISMANIC             E. Basic; at the roots
___ 6. PREFECTURAL            F. District administered or governed by a prefect
___ 7. SUPPURATED             G. Something coming forth from a source
___ 8. SOLICITOUS             H. Represented or appearing as such
___ 9. ATAVISTIC              I. Worn out; broken down from use
___10. BUFFETED               J. Conscious decision
___11. POMMELED               K. Producing the desired effect
___12. YEN                    L. Full of pus
___13. RUDIMENTARY            M. Decomposed, rotten, foul-smelling matter
___14. STUPEFIED              N. Unpredictable
___15. CATECHIST              O. Basic, central, or critical point
___16. REPUGNANT              P. Return of a trait after a period of absence
___17. DECREPIT               Q. Uncaring; uninterested
___18. CRUX                   R. Horrible; abominable; reprehensible
___19. EMANATION              S. Repulsive; disgusting; offensive
___20. OSTENSIBLY             T. Pulled out
___21. EFFACIOUS              U. One who teaches Christian doctrines
___22. HEINOUS                V. Japanese money
___23. PRECARIOUS             W. Dangerously lacking in security or stability
___24. VOLITION               X. Beat; hit
___25. EXTRICATED             Y. With senses dulled by amazement

Hiroshima Vocabulary Matching 2 Answer Key

| | | |
|---|---|---|
| B - 1. MALAISE | A. | Forced; battered |
| N - 2. CAPRICIOUS | B. | Sense of bodily discomfort, depression, or unease |
| M - 3. PUTRESCENCE | C. | Marked by anxious care and attentiveness |
| Q - 4. APATHETIC | D. | Magical |
| D - 5. TALISMANIC | E. | Basic; at the roots |
| F - 6. PREFECTURAL | F. | District administered or governed by a prefect |
| L - 7. SUPPURATED | G. | Something coming forth from a source |
| C - 8. SOLICITOUS | H. | Represented or appearing as such |
| P - 9. ATAVISTIC | I. | Worn out; broken down from use |
| A - 10. BUFFETED | J. | Conscious decision |
| X - 11. POMMELED | K. | Producing the desired effect |
| V - 12. YEN | L. | Full of pus |
| E - 13. RUDIMENTARY | M. | Decomposed, rotten, foul-smelling matter |
| Y - 14. STUPEFIED | N. | Unpredictable |
| U - 15. CATECHIST | O. | Basic, central, or critical point |
| S - 16. REPUGNANT | P. | Return of a trait after a period of absence |
| I - 17. DECREPIT | Q. | Uncaring; uninterested |
| O - 18. CRUX | R. | Horrible; abominable; reprehensible |
| G - 19. EMANATION | S. | Repulsive; disgusting; offensive |
| H - 20. OSTENSIBLY | T. | Pulled out |
| K - 21. EFFACIOUS | U. | One who teaches Christian doctrines |
| R - 22. HEINOUS | V. | Japanese money |
| W - 23. PRECARIOUS | W. | Dangerously lacking in security or stability |
| J - 24. VOLITION | X. | Beat; hit |
| T - 25. EXTRICATED | Y. | With senses dulled by amazement |

Hiroshima Vocabulary Matching 3

___ 1. PRECARIOUS        A. Something coming forth from a source
___ 2. POMMELED          B. One who teaches Christian doctrines
___ 3. CAPRICIOUS        C. Uncaring; uninterested
___ 4. DECREPIT          D. Unpredictable
___ 5. REPUGNANT         E. District administered or governed by a prefect
___ 6. PREFECTURAL       F. Conscious decision
___ 7. INTERMITTENT      G. Stopping and starting at intervals
___ 8. HEINOUS           H. Dangerously lacking in security or stability
___ 9. CONSECRATE        I. Of or containing chemicals that cause fire when exploded
___10. OSTENSIBLY        J. About to die
___11. PAROXYSM          K. Repulsive; disgusting; offensive
___12. MORIBUND          L. Pulled out
___13. STUPEFIED         M. Represented or appearing as such
___14. YEN               N. Sudden outburst
___15. CRUX              O. Worn out; broken down from use
___16. SOLICITOUS        P. Exploration of an area to gather information
___17. EMANATION         Q. Marked by anxious care and attentiveness
___18. EXTRICATED        R. Japanese money
___19. APATHETIC         S. Beat; hit
___20. ATTITUDINIZING    T. Horrible; abominable; reprehensible
___21. INCENDIARY        U. Assuming a false attitude; posturing
___22. RECONNAISSANCE    V. Full of pus
___23. VOLITION          W. Make sacred
___24. CATECHIST         X. With senses dulled by amazement
___25. SUPPURATED        Y. Basic, central, or critical point

Hiroshima Vocabulary Matching 3 Answer Key

| | | | |
|---|---|---|---|
| H - 1. | PRECARIOUS | A. | Something coming forth from a source |
| S - 2. | POMMELED | B. | One who teaches Christian doctrines |
| D - 3. | CAPRICIOUS | C. | Uncaring; uninterested |
| O - 4. | DECREPIT | D. | Unpredictable |
| K - 5. | REPUGNANT | E. | District administered or governed by a prefect |
| E - 6. | PREFECTURAL | F. | Conscious decision |
| G - 7. | INTERMITTENT | G. | Stopping and starting at intervals |
| T - 8. | HEINOUS | H. | Dangerously lacking in security or stability |
| W - 9. | CONSECRATE | I. | Of or containing chemicals that cause fire when exploded |
| M -10. | OSTENSIBLY | J. | About to die |
| N -11. | PAROXYSM | K. | Repulsive; disgusting; offensive |
| J -12. | MORIBUND | L. | Pulled out |
| X -13. | STUPEFIED | M. | Represented or appearing as such |
| R -14. | YEN | N. | Sudden outburst |
| Y -15. | CRUX | O. | Worn out; broken down from use |
| Q -16. | SOLICITOUS | P. | Exploration of an area to gather information |
| A -17. | EMANATION | Q. | Marked by anxious care and attentiveness |
| L -18. | EXTRICATED | R. | Japanese money |
| C -19. | APATHETIC | S. | Beat; hit |
| U -20. | ATTITUDINIZING | T. | Horrible; abominable; reprehensible |
| I -21. | INCENDIARY | U. | Assuming a false attitude; posturing |
| P -22. | RECONNAISSANCE | V. | Full of pus |
| F -23. | VOLITION | W. | Make sacred |
| B -24. | CATECHIST | X. | With senses dulled by amazement |
| V -25. | SUPPURATED | Y. | Basic, central, or critical point |

Hiroshima Vocabulary Matching 4

___ 1. SYBARITES  
___ 2. DECREPIT  
___ 3. PRECARIOUS  
___ 4. OSTENSIBLY  
___ 5. CONVIVIAL  
___ 6. EXTRICATED  
___ 7. TALISMANIC  
___ 8. ATAVISTIC  
___ 9. MORIBUND  
___ 10. SUPPURATED  
___ 11. CONTUSIONS  
___ 12. MALAISE  
___ 13. HEDONISTIC  
___ 14. PAROXYSM  
___ 15. YEN  
___ 16. STUPEFIED  
___ 17. INTERMITTENT  
___ 18. XENOPHOBIC  
___ 19. POMMELED  
___ 20. INCENDIARY  
___ 21. ATTITUDINIZING  
___ 22. RUDIMENTARY  
___ 23. CHAGRIN  
___ 24. APATHETIC  
___ 25. CHARRED  

A. Dangerously lacking in security or stability  
B. Magical  
C. Beat; hit  
D. Of or containing chemicals that cause fire when exploded  
E. With senses dulled by amazement  
F. Represented or appearing as such  
G. Sudden outburst  
H. Full of pus  
I. Feeling of embarrassment or humiliation caused by failure or disappointment  
J. Stopping and starting at intervals  
K. Sociable  
L. Uncaring; uninterested  
M. Sense of bodily discomfort, depression, or unease  
N. People devoted to pleasure and luxury  
O. Bruises  
P. Japanese money  
Q. Pulled out  
R. Characterized by the pursuit of sensual pleasure  
S. Scorched  
T. Basic; at the roots  
U. Worn out; broken down from use  
V. Return of a trait after a period of absence  
W. About to die  
X. Having a fear of foreigners  
Y. Assuming a false attitude; posturing

Hiroshima Vocabulary Matching 4 Answer Key

| | | |
|---|---|---|
| N - 1. SYBARITES | | A. Dangerously lacking in security or stability |
| U - 2. DECREPIT | | B. Magical |
| A - 3. PRECARIOUS | | C. Beat; hit |
| F - 4. OSTENSIBLY | | D. Of or containing chemicals that cause fire when exploded |
| K - 5. CONVIVIAL | | E. With senses dulled by amazement |
| Q - 6. EXTRICATED | | F. Represented or appearing as such |
| B - 7. TALISMANIC | | G. Sudden outburst |
| V - 8. ATAVISTIC | | H. Full of pus |
| W - 9. MORIBUND | | I. Feeling of embarrassment or humiliation caused by failure or disappointment |
| H - 10. SUPPURATED | | J. Stopping and starting at intervals |
| O - 11. CONTUSIONS | | K. Sociable |
| M - 12. MALAISE | | L. Uncaring; uninterested |
| R - 13. HEDONISTIC | | M. Sense of bodily discomfort, depression, or unease |
| G - 14. PAROXYSM | | N. People devoted to pleasure and luxury |
| P - 15. YEN | | O. Bruises |
| E - 16. STUPEFIED | | P. Japanese money |
| J - 17. INTERMITTENT | | Q. Pulled out |
| X - 18. XENOPHOBIC | | R. Characterized by the pursuit of sensual pleasure |
| C - 19. POMMELED | | S. Scorched |
| D - 20. INCENDIARY | | T. Basic; at the roots |
| Y - 21. ATTITUDINIZING | | U. Worn out; broken down from use |
| T - 22. RUDIMENTARY | | V. Return of a trait after a period of absence |
| I - 23. CHAGRIN | | W. About to die |
| L - 24. APATHETIC | | X. Having a fear of foreigners |
| S - 25. CHARRED | | Y. Assuming a false attitude; posturing |

Hiroshima Vocabulary Magic Squares 1

Match the definition with the vocabulary word. Put your answers in the magic squares below. When your answers are correct, all columns and rows will add to the same number.

A. CHARRED
B. APATHETIC
C. OSTENSIBLY
D. ATAVISTIC
E. PREFECTURAL
F. ATTITUDINIZING
G. RECONNAISSANCE
H. RUDIMENTARY
I. CHAGRIN
J. HEDONISTIC
K. SUCCINCT
L. PRECARIOUS
M. SUPPURATED
N. BUFFETED
O. MORIBUND
P. EMANATION

1. About to die
2. Return of a trait after a period of absence
3. Characterized by the pursuit of sensual pleasure
4. District administered or governed by a prefect
5. Feeling of embarrassment or humiliation caused by failure or disappointment
6. Assuming a false attitude; posturing
7. Something coming forth from a source
8. Represented or appearing as such
9. Basic; at the roots
10. Short and to the point
11. Scorched
12. Forced; battered
13. Uncaring; uninterested
14. Full of pus
15. Exploration of an area to gather information
16. Dangerously lacking in security or stability

| A= | B= | C= | D= |
|---|---|---|---|
| E= | F= | G= | H= |
| I= | J= | K= | L= |
| M= | N= | O= | P= |

Hiroshima Vocabulary Magic Squares 1 Answer Key

Match the definition with the vocabulary word. Put your answers in the magic squares below. When your answers are correct, all columns and rows will add to the same number.

A. CHARRED
B. APATHETIC
C. OSTENSIBLY
D. ATAVISTIC
E. PREFECTURAL
F. ATTITUDINIZING
G. RECONNAISSANCE
H. RUDIMENTARY
I. CHAGRIN
J. HEDONISTIC
K. SUCCINCT
L. PRECARIOUS
M. SUPPURATED
N. BUFFETED
O. MORIBUND
P. EMANATION

1. About to die
2. Return of a trait after a period of absence
3. Characterized by the pursuit of sensual pleasure
4. District administered or governed by a prefect
5. Feeling of embarrassment or humiliation caused by failure or disappointment
6. Assuming a false attitude; posturing
7. Something coming forth from a source
8. Represented or appearing as such
9. Basic; at the roots
10. Short and to the point
11. Scorched
12. Forced; battered
13. Uncaring; uninterested
14. Full of pus
15. Exploration of an area to gather information
16. Dangerously lacking in security or stability

| A=11 | B=13 | C=8 | D=2 |
| --- | --- | --- | --- |
| E=4 | F=6 | G=15 | H=9 |
| I=5 | J=3 | K=10 | L=16 |
| M=14 | N=12 | O=1 | P=7 |

Hiroshima Vocabulary Magic Squares 2

Match the definition with the vocabulary word. Put your answers in the magic squares below. When your answers are correct, all columns and rows will add to the same number.

A. SYBARITES
B. YEN
C. APATHETIC
D. REPUGNANT
E. PREFECTURAL
F. CHAGRIN
G. HEDONISTIC
H. CAPRICIOUS
I. CONTUSIONS
J. OSTENSIBLY
K. POMMELED
L. ATAVISTIC
M. CONVIVIAL
N. SOLICITOUS
O. BREVIARY
P. INTERMITTENT

1. People devoted to pleasure and luxury
2. Marked by anxious care and attentiveness
3. Represented or appearing as such
4. District administered or governed by a prefect
5. Characterized by the pursuit of sensual pleasure
6. Return of a trait after a period of absence
7. Stopping and starting at intervals
8. Uncaring; uninterested
9. Book containing hymns and prayers
10. Repulsive; disgusting; offensive
11. Unpredictable
12. Beat; hit
13. Bruises
14. Feeling of embarrassment or humiliation caused by failure or disappointment
15. Japanese money
16. Sociable

| A= | B= | C= | D= |
| E= | F= | G= | H= |
| I= | J= | K= | L= |
| M= | N= | O= | P= |

Hiroshima Vocabulary Magic Squares 2 Answer Key

Match the definition with the vocabulary word. Put your answers in the magic squares below. When your answers are correct, all columns and rows will add to the same number.

A. SYBARITES
B. YEN
C. APATHETIC
D. REPUGNANT
E. PREFECTURAL
F. CHAGRIN
G. HEDONISTIC
H. CAPRICIOUS
I. CONTUSIONS
J. OSTENSIBLY
K. POMMELED
L. ATAVISTIC
M. CONVIVIAL
N. SOLICITOUS
O. BREVIARY
P. INTERMITTENT

1. People devoted to pleasure and luxury
2. Marked by anxious care and attentiveness
3. Represented or appearing as such
4. District administered or governed by a prefect
5. Characterized by the pursuit of sensual pleasure
6. Return of a trait after a period of absence
7. Stopping and starting at intervals
8. Uncaring; uninterested
9. Book containing hymns and prayers
10. Repulsive; disgusting; offensive
11. Unpredictable
12. Beat; hit
13. Bruises
14. Feeling of embarrassment or humiliation caused by failure or disappointment
15. Japanese money
16. Sociable

| A=1 | B=15 | C=8 | D=10 |
| --- | --- | --- | --- |
| E=4 | F=14 | G=5 | H=11 |
| I=13 | J=3 | K=12 | L=6 |
| M=16 | N=2 | O=9 | P=7 |

Hiroshima Vocabulary Magic Squares 3

Match the definition with the vocabulary word. Put your answers in the magic squares below. When your answers are correct, all columns and rows will add to the same number.

A. CONTUSIONS
B. CAPRICIOUS
C. YEN
D. DECREPIT
E. RECONNAISSANCE
F. PRECARIOUS
G. SUCCINCT
H. VOLITION
I. EMANATION
J. RUDIMENTARY
K. BREVIARY
L. POMMELED
M. APATHETIC
N. CONVIVIAL
O. PREFECTURAL
P. CATECHIST

1. Dangerously lacking in security or stability
2. Something coming forth from a source
3. District administered or governed by a prefect
4. Worn out; broken down from use
5. Uncaring; uninterested
6. Unpredictable
7. Conscious decision
8. Book containing hymns and prayers
9. Japanese money
10. One who teaches Christian doctrines
11. Basic; at the roots
12. Exploration of an area to gather information
13. Beat; hit
14. Short and to the point
15. Bruises
16. Sociable

| A= | B= | C= | D= |
| E= | F= | G= | H= |
| I= | J= | K= | L= |
| M= | N= | O= | P= |

Hiroshima Vocabulary Magic Squares 3 Answer Key

Match the definition with the vocabulary word. Put your answers in the magic squares below. When your answers are correct, all columns and rows will add to the same number.

A. CONTUSIONS
B. CAPRICIOUS
C. YEN
D. DECREPIT
E. RECONNAISSANCE
F. PRECARIOUS

G. SUCCINCT
H. VOLITION
I. EMANATION
J. RUDIMENTARY
K. BREVIARY
L. POMMELED

M. APATHETIC
N. CONVIVIAL
O. PREFECTURAL
P. CATECHIST

1. Dangerously lacking in security or stability
2. Something coming forth from a source
3. District administered or governed by a prefect
4. Worn out; broken down from use
5. Uncaring; uninterested
6. Unpredictable
7. Conscious decision
8. Book containing hymns and prayers
9. Japanese money
10. One who teaches Christian doctrines
11. Basic; at the roots
12. Exploration of an area to gather information
13. Beat; hit
14. Short and to the point
15. Bruises
16. Sociable

| A=15 | B=6 | C=9 | D=4 |
| --- | --- | --- | --- |
| E=12 | F=1 | G=14 | H=7 |
| I=2 | J=11 | K=8 | L=13 |
| M=5 | N=16 | O=3 | P=10 |

Hiroshima Vocabulary Magic Squares 4

Match the definition with the vocabulary word. Put your answers in the magic squares below. When your answers are correct, all columns and rows will add to the same number.

A. VOLITION
B. SYBARITES
C. RUDIMENTARY
D. CONVIVIAL
E. SUPPURATED
F. STUPEFIED
G. DECREPIT
H. MIASMA
I. BREVIARY
J. REPUGNANT
K. PRECARIOUS
L. MORIBUND
M. PREFECTURAL
N. HEDONISTIC
O. OSTENSIBLY
P. CAPRICIOUS

1. Poisonous atmosphere
2. Conscious decision
3. People devoted to pleasure and luxury
4. Worn out; broken down from use
5. Repulsive; disgusting; offensive
6. Represented or appearing as such
7. Unpredictable
8. Book containing hymns and prayers
9. Dangerously lacking in security or stability
10. Characterized by the pursuit of sensual pleasure
11. District administered or governed by a prefect
12. About to die
13. Full of pus
14. Sociable
15. Basic; at the roots
16. With senses dulled by amazement

| A= | B= | C= | D= |
| E= | F= | G= | H= |
| I= | J= | K= | L= |
| M= | N= | O= | P= |

Hiroshima Vocabulary Magic Squares 4 Answer Key

Match the definition with the vocabulary word. Put your answers in the magic squares below. When your answers are correct, all columns and rows will add to the same number.

A. VOLITION
B. SYBARITES
C. RUDIMENTARY
D. CONVIVIAL
E. SUPPURATED
F. STUPEFIED
G. DECREPIT
H. MIASMA
I. BREVIARY
J. REPUGNANT
K. PRECARIOUS
L. MORIBUND
M. PREFECTURAL
N. HEDONISTIC
O. OSTENSIBLY
P. CAPRICIOUS

1. Poisonous atmosphere
2. Conscious decision
3. People devoted to pleasure and luxury
4. Worn out; broken down from use
5. Repulsive; disgusting; offensive
6. Represented or appearing as such
7. Unpredictable
8. Book containing hymns and prayers
9. Dangerously lacking in security or stability
10. Characterized by the pursuit of sensual pleasure
11. District administered or governed by a prefect
12. About to die
13. Full of pus
14. Sociable
15. Basic; at the roots
16. With senses dulled by amazement

| A=2 | B=3 | C=15 | D=14 |
| --- | --- | --- | --- |
| E=13 | F=16 | G=4 | H=1 |
| I=8 | J=5 | K=9 | L=12 |
| M=11 | N=10 | O=6 | P=7 |

# Hiroshima Vocabulary Word Search 1

Words are placed backwards, forward, diagonally, up and down. Clues listed below can help you find the words. Circle the hidden vocabulary words in the maze.

```
H M A L A I S E X D C C O N V I V I A L
R E G Z S V F M E P R H I L S H T N Y X
U V D F T L D T N Q P R A E B I W T D V
D E Z O B Z E F O X G L T R P T Y E P P
I P X F N F R L P A N I M E R L L R Y B
M T D T F I N S H V R X R G B E E M P Z
E S H U R C S C O A Y C X I M F D I U J
N I B L M I P T B L E S S M E F S T T Z
T H P F P R C Y I D W N O C R A F T R B
A C H C D H S A C C E P T K E C W E E T
R E D Z A K G K T T R U J F P I T N S X
Y T M C Z P S H S E R L P R U O D T C J
L A X A O G R O V A D Y G H G U N S E D
Q C W Q N N B I L O S B Y K N S U U N L
P Z R V M A T P C F L Z N E A O B C C Q
T H A T T I T U D I N I Z I N G I C E R
V X V M Q Q A I S S O Z T I T C R I X M
Q U H J Q G N S O I T U E I D V O N Y L
B R E V I A R Y M N O H S G O F M C N N
P C I T E H T A P A J N S F N N K T L T
A T A V I S T I C C O N S E C R A T E V
```

About to die (8)
Assuming a false attitude; posturing (14)
Basic, central, or critical point (4)
Basic; at the roots (11)
Beat; hit (8)
Book containing hymns and prayers (8)
Bruises (10)
Characterized by the pursuit of sensual pleasure (10)
Conscious decision (8)
Decomposed, rotten, foul-smelling matter (11)
District administered or governed by a prefect (11)
Feeling of embarrassment or humiliation caused by failure or disappointment (7)
Forced; battered (8)
Having a fear of foreigners (10)
Horrible; abominable; reprehensible (7)
Japanese money (3)

Make sacred (10)
One who teaches Christian doctrines (9)
People devoted to pleasure and luxury (9)
Poisonous atmosphere (6)
Producing the desired effect (9)
Pulled out (10)
Represented or appearing as such (10)
Repulsive; disgusting; offensive (9)
Return of a trait after a period of absence (9)
Scorched (7)
Sense of bodily discomfort, depression, or unease (7)
Short and to the point (8)
Sociable (9)
Something coming forth from a source (9)
Stopping and starting at intervals (12)
Uncaring; uninterested (9)
Unpredictable (10)
Worn out; broken down from use (8)

Hiroshima Vocabulary Word Search 1 Answer Key

Words are placed backwards, forward, diagonally, up and down. Clues listed below can help you find the words. Circle the hidden vocabulary words in the maze.

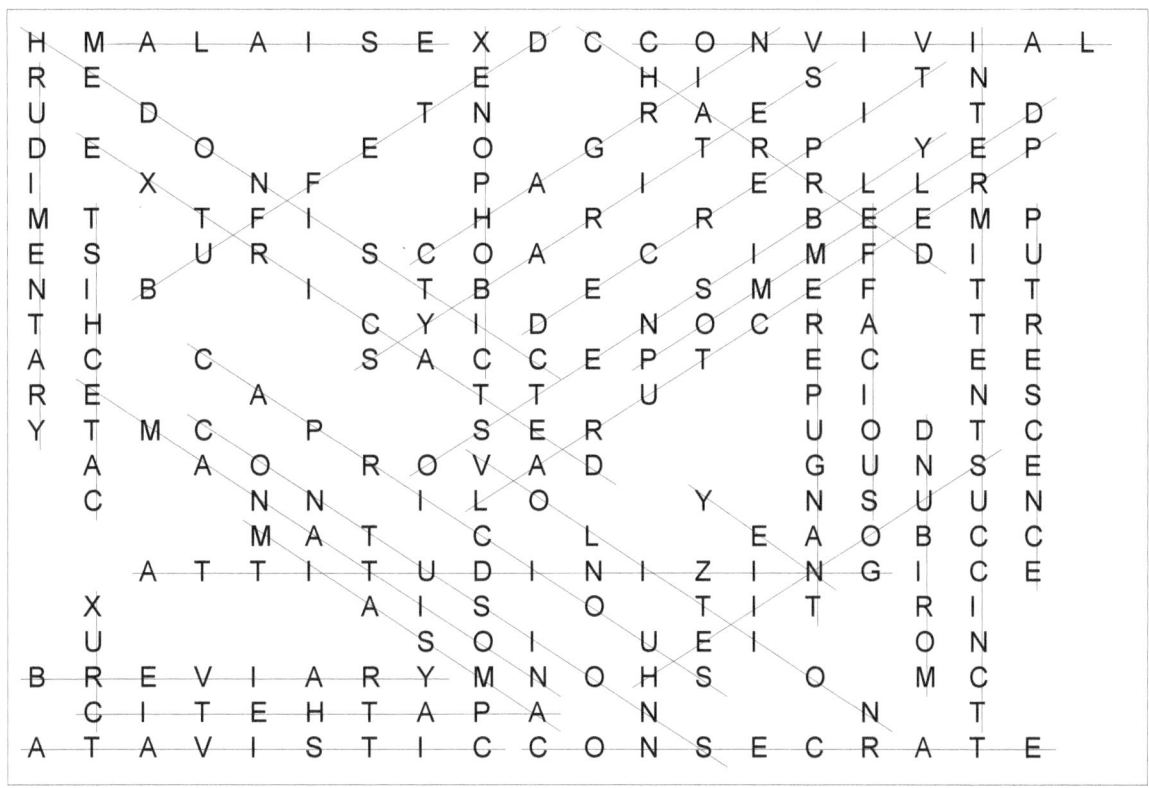

About to die (8)
Assuming a false attitude; posturing (14)
Basic, central, or critical point (4)
Basic; at the roots (11)
Beat; hit (8)
Book containing hymns and prayers (8)
Bruises (10)
Characterized by the pursuit of sensual pleasure (10)
Conscious decision (8)
Decomposed, rotten, foul-smelling matter (11)
District administered or governed by a prefect (11)
Feeling of embarrassment or humiliation caused by failure or disappointment (7)
Forced; battered (8)
Having a fear of foreigners (10)
Horrible; abominable; reprehensible (7)
Japanese money (3)

Make sacred (10)
One who teaches Christian doctrines (9)
People devoted to pleasure and luxury (9)
Poisonous atmosphere (6)
Producing the desired effect (9)
Pulled out (10)
Represented or appearing as such (10)
Repulsive; disgusting; offensive (9)
Return of a trait after a period of absence (9)
Scorched (7)
Sense of bodily discomfort, depression, or unease (7)
Short and to the point (8)
Sociable (9)
Something coming forth from a source (9)
Stopping and starting at intervals (12)
Uncaring; uninterested (9)
Unpredictable (10)
Worn out; broken down from use (8)

Hiroshima Vocabulary Word Search 2

Words are placed backwards, forward, diagonally, up and down. Clues listed below can help you find the words. Circle the hidden vocabulary words in the maze.

```
S T U P E F I E D R U D I M E N T A R Y
Q E T N E T T I M R E T N I Y Q K H M P
C M C A P R I C I O U S J E V V W P O Y
C A M R L U X S N O I S U T N O C R R X
R N T L C I T S I V A T A A B L O E I G
H A P E R M S R H L V B G R R A N P B S
H T M N C K O M E C J G H C E R V U U L
J I A Q H H L B A S V Z K E V U I G N V
H O L T L K I P X N C P Z S I T V N D N
E N A H T X C S O C I E D N A C I A H D
I C I F Z I I I T N Z C N O R E A N E M
N S S C X N T N I R G A H C Y F L T P X
O Y E S E I O U Q E M D I R E E A C A Q
U B H Y L B U B D S F B F U T R Y N R H
S A B O F U S C A I O F J X U P K I O Q
L R V V D F C I H H N S A P C R R C X J
N I S N Q F M Y P A G I P C V Y H C Y N
W T K X C E Z O F Y R U Z Y I K T U S T
N E S F D T N M F G S R K I J O J S M Q
Y S O S T E N S I B L Y E H N W U W Q Z
Q V X Y X D E L E M M O P D L G G S R Y
```

About to die (8)
Assuming a false attitude; posturing (14)
Basic, central, or critical point (4)
Basic; at the roots (11)
Beat; hit (8)
Book containing hymns and prayers (8)
Bruises (10)
Conscious decision (8)
Decomposed, rotten, foul-smelling matter (11)
District administered or governed by a prefect (11)
Feeling of embarrassment or humiliation caused by failure or disappointment (7)
Forced; battered (8)
Full of pus (10)
Having a fear of foreigners (10)
Horrible; abominable; reprehensible (7)
Japanese money (3)
Magical (10)

Make sacred (10)
Marked by anxious care and attentiveness (10)
One who teaches Christian doctrines (9)
People devoted to pleasure and luxury (9)
Poisonous atmosphere (6)
Producing the desired effect (9)
Represented or appearing as such (10)
Repulsive; disgusting; offensive (9)
Return of a trait after a period of absence (9)
Scorched (7)
Sense of bodily discomfort, depression, or unease (7)
Short and to the point (8)
Sociable (9)
Something coming forth from a source (9)
Stopping and starting at intervals (12)
Sudden outburst (8)
Unpredictable (10)
With senses dulled by amazement (9)

Hiroshima Vocabulary Word Search 2 Answer Key

Words are placed backwards, forward, diagonally, up and down. Clues listed below can help you find the words. Circle the hidden vocabulary words in the maze.

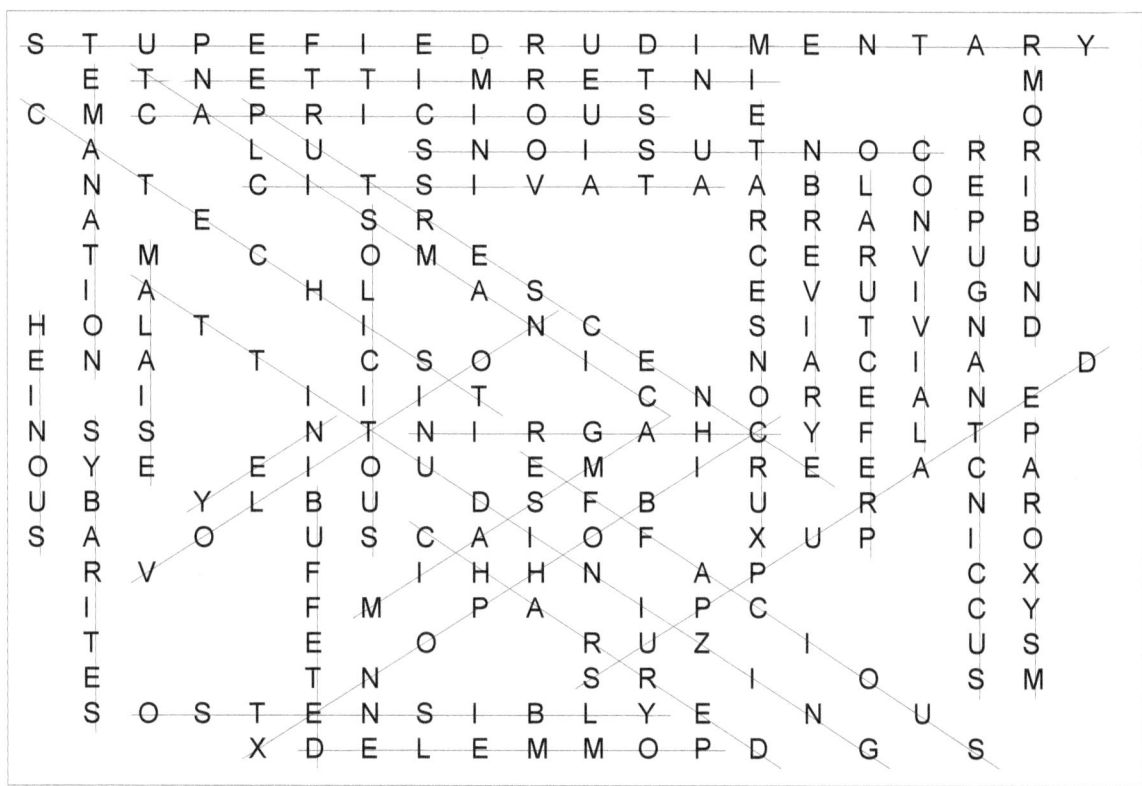

About to die (8)
Assuming a false attitude; posturing (14)
Basic, central, or critical point (4)
Basic; at the roots (11)
Beat; hit (8)
Book containing hymns and prayers (8)
Bruises (10)
Conscious decision (8)
Decomposed, rotten, foul-smelling matter (11)
District administered or governed by a prefect (11)
Feeling of embarrassment or humiliation caused by failure or disappointment (7)
Forced; battered (8)
Full of pus (10)
Having a fear of foreigners (10)
Horrible; abominable; reprehensible (7)
Japanese money (3)
Magical (10)
Make sacred (10)
Marked by anxious care and attentiveness (10)
One who teaches Christian doctrines (9)
People devoted to pleasure and luxury (9)
Poisonous atmosphere (6)
Producing the desired effect (9)
Represented or appearing as such (10)
Repulsive; disgusting; offensive (9)
Return of a trait after a period of absence (9)
Scorched (7)
Sense of bodily discomfort, depression, or unease (7)
Short and to the point (8)
Sociable (9)
Something coming forth from a source (9)
Stopping and starting at intervals (12)
Sudden outburst (8)
Unpredictable (10)
With senses dulled by amazement (9)

Hiroshima Vocabulary Word Search 3

Words are placed backwards, forward, diagonally, up and down. Words listed below are included in the maze. Circle the hidden vocabulary words in the maze.

```
R U D I M E N T A R Y F P S P V X Q F M
E X E N O P H O B I C R U D Z O T G L J
T N A N G U P E R M E O E V V L K H S X
A L R C D S J H S C I T V S Q I L O L J
R V D B D S X Y A C A Z M K N T L W B S
C B E M G N X R I C O N T U S I O N S K
E W C N F O I R I X X R K M C O N U U F
S G R R R O P R Q R P E C I L N O S O K
N U E A U A T Q C N Z C T L A N I U I F
O S P S C X X I E C D O H E I M T C C N
C S I P E H T Y I P U N C E V O A C A S
S B T K U S A T N S H N H C I R N I F T
V Y H E I R E G C J E A A A V I A N F R
B Z B V N H A Y R C D I R T N B M C E N
M U A A T S R T S I O S R E O U E T K E
R T F A R A I E E A N S E C C N R T S T
A C P F I I R B M D I A D H R D J I M Y
G A C V E T T S L Y S N W I B Y A J V H
D M E S U T A E J Y T C V S X L V N P D
K R Y P S I E N S W I E Z T A H V C C X
B T F B M P V D F F C P O M M E L E D J
```

| APATHETIC | DECREPIT | PRECARIOUS |
| ATAVISTIC | EFFACIOUS | PUTRESCENCE |
| BREVIARY | EMANATION | RECONNAISSANCE |
| BUFFETED | EXTRICATED | REPUGNANT |
| CAPRICIOUS | HEDONISTIC | RUDIMENTARY |
| CATECHIST | HEINOUS | SOLICITOUS |
| CHAGRIN | MALAISE | SUCCINCT |
| CHARRED | MIASMA | SUPPURATED |
| CONSECRATE | MORIBUND | SYBARITES |
| CONTUSIONS | OSTENSIBLY | VOLITION |
| CONVIVIAL | PAROXYSM | XENOPHOBIC |
| CRUX | POMMELED | YEN |

Hiroshima Vocabulary Word Search 3 Answer Key

Words are placed backwards, forward, diagonally, up and down. Words listed below are included in the maze. Circle the hidden vocabulary words in the maze.

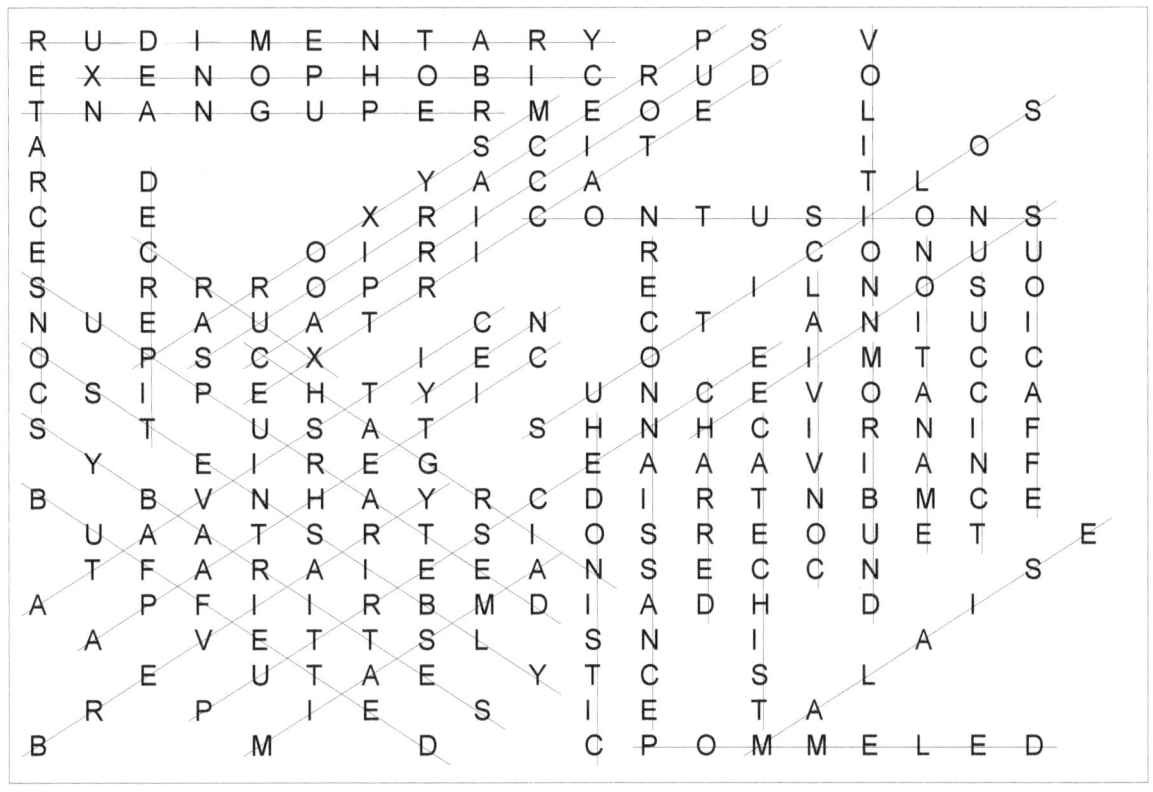

| APATHETIC | DECREPIT | PRECARIOUS |
| ATAVISTIC | EFFACIOUS | PUTRESCENCE |
| BREVIARY | EMANATION | RECONNAISSANCE |
| BUFFETED | EXTRICATED | REPUGNANT |
| CAPRICIOUS | HEDONISTIC | RUDIMENTARY |
| CATECHIST | HEINOUS | SOLICITOUS |
| CHAGRIN | MALAISE | SUCCINCT |
| CHARRED | MIASMA | SUPPURATED |
| CONSECRATE | MORIBUND | SYBARITES |
| CONTUSIONS | OSTENSIBLY | VOLITION |
| CONVIVIAL | PAROXYSM | XENOPHOBIC |
| CRUX | POMMELED | YEN |

# Hiroshima Vocabulary Word Search 4

Words are placed backwards, forward, diagonally, up and down. Words listed below are included in the maze. Circle the hidden vocabulary words in the maze.

```
T A L I S M A N I C B R E V I A R Y P J
R S D N T F X X L A R U T C E F E R P S
Z T C C N S P G M Q F Z D P X S M A F K
L U O E A B U F F E T E D S T U Y T G Y
B P N N N P N P W C C D P T R C S N Y N
V E T D G T R J P R H L G M I C U E H D
E F U I U Z Z I E U R A M W C I O M H N
C I S A P H G P C N R Q R W A N T I W I
N E I R E R I W Z I L A C R T C I D Q R
E D O Y R T Q D N T O M T V E T C U H G
C V N V F T E O S M W U C E D D I R H A
S J S L T L I I T G E R S Z D A L N E H
E C G M E T H V N F X E N O P H O B I C
R D O M A C C W F W G M N A M I S B N Y
T W M N E T J A M M S P T S T X Z K O T
U O A T V M C M N S V H Y I F S K J U S
P M A L A I S E Z V E X L Y C R U X S K
E C B R O A V V L T O O B E C P L T X D
F C P U Y S B I I R V R D N U B I R O M
M W S D J M F C A A T A V I S T I C P V
Z R T S Z A Q P G L S Y B A R I T E S S
```

| APATHETIC | CONVIVIAL | MIASMA | STUPEFIED |
| ATAVISTIC | CRUX | MORIBUND | SUCCINCT |
| BREVIARY | DECREPIT | PAROXYSM | SUPPURATED |
| BUFFETED | EFFACIOUS | POMMELED | SYBARITES |
| CAPRICIOUS | EMANATION | PREFECTURAL | TALISMANIC |
| CATECHIST | EXTRICATED | PUTRESCENCE | VOLITION |
| CHAGRIN | HEINOUS | REPUGNANT | XENOPHOBIC |
| CHARRED | INCENDIARY | RUDIMENTARY | YEN |
| CONTUSIONS | MALAISE | SOLICITOUS | |

Hiroshima Vocabulary Word Search 4 Answer Key

Words are placed backwards, forward, diagonally, up and down. Words listed below are included in the maze. Circle the hidden vocabulary words in the maze.

| APATHETIC | CONVIVIAL | MIASMA | STUPEFIED |
| ATAVISTIC | CRUX | MORIBUND | SUCCINCT |
| BREVIARY | DECREPIT | PAROXYSM | SUPPURATED |
| BUFFETED | EFFACIOUS | POMMELED | SYBARITES |
| CAPRICIOUS | EMANATION | PREFECTURAL | TALISMANIC |
| CATECHIST | EXTRICATED | PUTRESCENCE | VOLITION |
| CHAGRIN | HEINOUS | REPUGNANT | XENOPHOBIC |
| CHARRED | INCENDIARY | RUDIMENTARY | YEN |
| CONTUSIONS | MALAISE | SOLICITOUS | |

Hiroshima Vocabulary Crossword 1

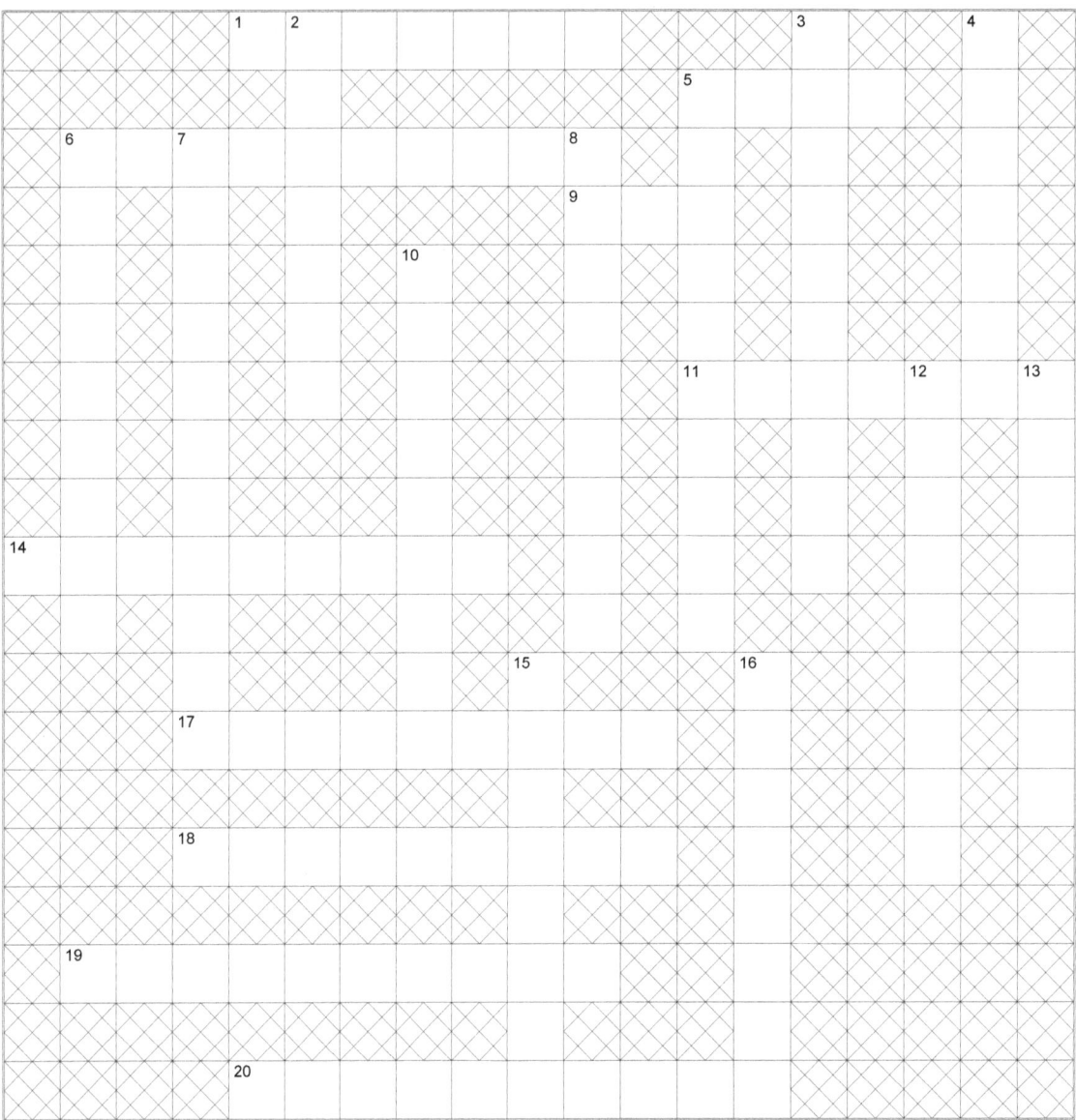

Across
1. Feeling of embarrassment or humiliation caused by failure or disappointment
5. Basic, central, or critical point
6. Unpredictable
9. Japanese money
11. Scorched
14. One who teaches Christian doctrines
17. Producing the desired effect
18. Something coming forth from a source
19. Dangerously lacking in security or stability
20. Of or containing chemicals that cause fire when exploded

Down
2. Horrible; abominable; reprehensible
3. Full of pus
4. Sense of bodily discomfort, depression, or unease
5. Make sacred
6. Sociable
7. Decomposed, rotten, foul-smelling matter
8. People devoted to pleasure and luxury
10. Return of a trait after a period of absence
12. Repulsive; disgusting; offensive
13. Worn out; broken down from use
15. About to die
16. Book containing hymns and prayers

# Hiroshima Vocabulary Crossword 1 Answer Key

|   |   |   | ¹C | ²H | A | G | R | I | N |   |   | ³S |   | ⁴M |
|---|---|---|----|----|---|---|---|---|---|---|---|----|---|----|
|   |   |   |    | E  |   |   |   |   |   |   | ⁵C | R  | U | X  | A |
| ⁶C | A | ⁷P | R | I | C | I | O | U | ⁸S |   | O  | P  |   | L  |
| O |   | U |   | N |   |   |   |   | ⁹Y | E | N  | P  |   | A  |
| N |   | T |   | O |   | ¹⁰A |   |   | B |   | S  | U  |   | I  |
| V |   | R |   | U |   | T  |   |   | A |   | E  | R  |   | S  |
| I |   | E |   | S |   | A  |   |   | R |   | ¹¹C | H | A | ¹²R | ¹³E | D |
| V |   | S |   |   |   | V  |   |   | I |   | R  | T |   | E  | E |
| I |   | C |   |   |   | I  |   |   | T |   | A  | E |   | P  | C |
| ¹⁴C | A | T | E | C | H | I | S | T |   | E |   | T | D |    | U | R |
|   |   | L |   | N |   |   | T |   |   | S |   | E |   |    | G | E |
|   |   |   |   | C |   |   | I |   | ¹⁵M |   | ¹⁶B |   |   |    | N | P |
|   |   |   |   | ¹⁷E | F | F | A | C | I | O | U | S | R |   |    | A | I |
|   |   |   |   |    |   |   |   |   | R |   |   | E |   |   |    | N | T |
|   |   |   |   | ¹⁸E | M | A | N | A | T | I | O | N | V |   |    | T |   |
|   |   |   |   |    |   |   |   |   | B |   |   | I |   |   |    |   |   |
|   |   | ¹⁹P | R | E | C | A | R | I | O | U | S |   | A |   |    |   |   |
|   |   |    |   |    |   |   |   |   | N |   |   |   | R |   |    |   |   |
|   |   |    |   | ²⁰I | N | C | E | N | D | I | A | R | Y |   |    |   |   |

Across
1. Feeling of embarrassment or humiliation caused by failure or disappointment
5. Basic, central, or critical point
6. Unpredictable
9. Japanese money
11. Scorched
14. One who teaches Christian doctrines
17. Producing the desired effect
18. Something coming forth from a source
19. Dangerously lacking in security or stability
20. Of or containing chemicals that cause fire when exploded

Down
2. Horrible; abominable; reprehensible
3. Full of pus
4. Sense of bodily discomfort, depression, or unease
5. Make sacred
6. Sociable
7. Decomposed, rotten, foul-smelling matter
8. People devoted to pleasure and luxury
10. Return of a trait after a period of absence
12. Repulsive; disgusting; offensive
13. Worn out; broken down from use
15. About to die
16. Book containing hymns and prayers

Hiroshima Vocabulary Crossword 2

Across
1. Book containing hymns and prayers
5. Worn out; broken down from use
8. Stopping and starting at intervals
10. Forced; battered
11. Short and to the point
12. Uncaring; uninterested
16. Japanese money
20. Repulsive; disgusting; offensive
21. People devoted to pleasure and luxury
22. Horrible; abominable; reprehensible
23. Characterized by the pursuit of sensual pleasure

Down
2. Basic; at the roots
3. Of or containing chemicals that cause fire when exploded
4. About to die
6. Pulled out
7. Producing the desired effect
9. Poisonous atmosphere
13. Sudden outburst
14. Basic, central, or critical point
15. Scorched
17. Something coming forth from a source
18. Sociable
19. Feeling of embarrassment or humiliation caused by failure or disappointment

# Hiroshima Vocabulary Crossword 2 Answer Key

|   |   | 1 B | 2 R | E | 3 I | A | R | Y |   |   |   |   |   |
|---|---|---|---|---|---|---|---|---|---|---|---|---|---|
| 4 M |   |   | U |   | N |   |   |   | 5 D | 6 E | C | R | E | P | I | T |
| O |   |   | D |   | C |   |   |   |   | X |   |   |   |
| R |   | 7 E | 8 I | N | T | E | R | 9 M | I | T | T | E | N | T |
| I |   | F |   M |   |   | N |   | I |   | R |   |   |   |
| 10 B | U | F | F | E | T | E | D | A |   | I |   |   |   |
| U |   | A |   | N |   | I |   | 11 S | U | C | C | I | N | C | T |
| N |   | C |   | T |   | A |   | M |   | A |   |   |   |
| D |   | I |   | A |   | R |   | 12 A | 13 P | A | T | H | E | T | I | 14 C |
|   |   | O |   | R |   | Y |   | A |   | E |   |   |   | R |
| 15 C |   | U |   | 16 Y | 17 E | N |   | R |   | D |   | 18 C |   | U |
| H |   | S |   |   | M |   |   | O |   |   |   | O |   | X |
| A |   |   |   |   | A |   |   | X |   | 19 C |   | N |   |
| 20 R | E | P | U | G | N | A | N | T |   | H |   | V |   |
| R |   |   |   |   | A |   |   | 21 S | Y | B | A | R | I | T | E | S |
| E |   |   |   |   | T |   |   | M |   | G |   | V |   |
| D |   |   | 22 H | E | I | N | O | U | S |   | R |   | I |
|   |   |   |   | O |   |   |   |   |   | I |   | A |
|   | 23 H | E | D | O | N | I | S | T | I | C |   | N |   | L |

### Across
1. Book containing hymns and prayers
5. Worn out; broken down from use
8. Stopping and starting at intervals
10. Forced; battered
11. Short and to the point
12. Uncaring; uninterested
16. Japanese money
20. Repulsive; disgusting; offensive
21. People devoted to pleasure and luxury
22. Horrible; abominable; reprehensible
23. Characterized by the pursuit of sensual pleasure

### Down
2. Basic; at the roots
3. Of or containing chemicals that cause fire when exploded
4. About to die
6. Pulled out
7. Producing the desired effect
9. Poisonous atmosphere
13. Sudden outburst
14. Basic, central, or critical point
15. Scorched
17. Something coming forth from a source
18. Sociable
19. Feeling of embarrassment or humiliation caused by failure or disappointment

Hiroshima Vocabulary Crossword 3

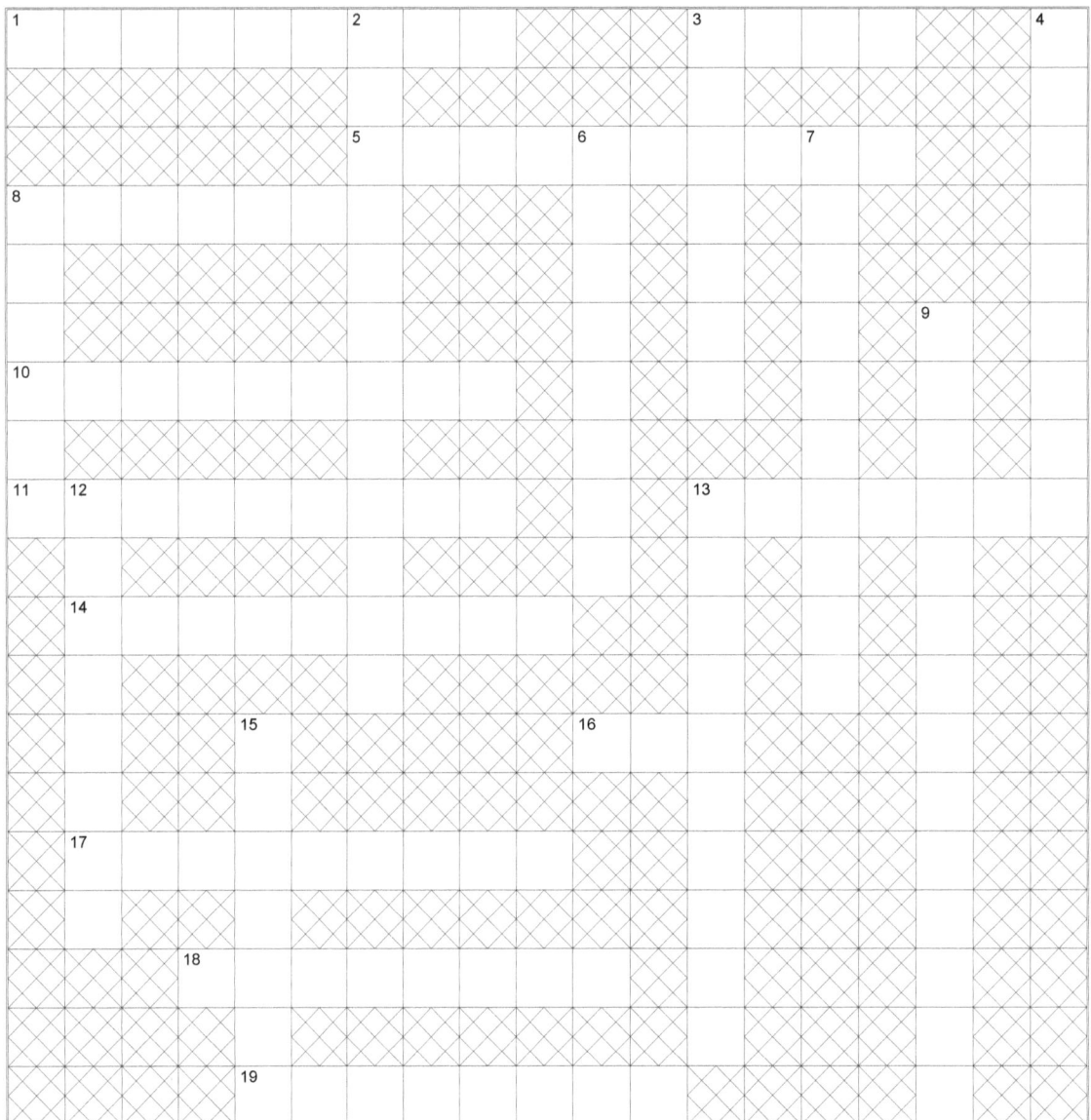

Across
1. Sociable
3. Basic, central, or critical point
5. Magical
8. Sense of bodily discomfort, depression, or unease
10. With senses dulled by amazement
11. Uncaring; uninterested
13. Horrible; abominable; reprehensible
14. Repulsive; disgusting; offensive
16. Japanese money
17. People devoted to pleasure and luxury
18. Book containing hymns and prayers
19. Worn out; broken down from use

Down
2. Stopping and starting at intervals
3. Feeling of embarrassment or humiliation caused by failure or disappointment
4. Producing the desired effect
6. Short and to the point
7. Of or containing chemicals that cause fire when exploded
8. Poisonous atmosphere
9. Exploration of an area to gather information
12. Sudden outburst
13. Characterized by the pursuit of sensual pleasure
15. Scorched

# Hiroshima Vocabulary Crossword 3 Answer Key

|   |   |   |   |   |   |   |   |   |   |   |   |   |   |
|---|---|---|---|---|---|---|---|---|---|---|---|---|---|
| ¹C | O | N | V | I | ²I | A | L |   | ³C | R | U | X | ⁴E |
|   |   |   |   |   | N |   |   |   | H |   |   |   | F |
|   |   |   |   |   | ⁵T | A | L | ⁶I | S | M | A | N | ⁷I | C |   | F |
| ⁸M | A | L | A | I | S | E |   |   | U |   | G |   | N |   | A |
| I |   |   |   |   | R |   |   |   | C |   | R |   | C |   | C |
| A |   |   |   |   | M |   |   |   | C |   | I |   | E | ⁹R | I |
| ¹⁰S | T | U | P | E | F | I | E | D |   | I |   | N |   | D | E | O |
| M |   |   |   |   | T |   |   |   |   | N |   |   | D |   | C | U |
| ¹¹A | ¹²P | A | T | H | E | T | I | C |   | C |   | ¹³H | E | I | N | O | U | S |
|   | A |   |   |   | E |   |   |   |   | T |   | E |   | A |   | N |
|   | ¹⁴R | E | P | U | G | N | A | N | T |   |   | D |   | R |   | N |
|   | O |   |   |   | T |   |   |   |   |   |   | O |   | Y |   | A |
|   | X |   |   | ¹⁵C |   |   |   | ¹⁶Y | E | N |   |   |   |   |   | I |
|   | Y |   |   | H |   |   |   |   |   | I |   |   |   |   |   | S |
|   | ¹⁷S | Y | B | A | R | I | T | E | S |   | S |   |   |   |   | S |
|   | M |   |   | R |   |   |   |   |   | T |   |   |   |   | A |
|   |   |   | ¹⁸B | R | E | V | I | A | R | Y | I |   |   |   | N |
|   |   |   |   | E |   |   |   |   |   |   | C |   |   |   | C |
|   |   |   | ¹⁹D | E | C | R | E | P | I | T |   |   |   |   | E |

### Across
1. Sociable
3. Basic, central, or critical point
5. Magical
8. Sense of bodily discomfort, depression, or unease
10. With senses dulled by amazement
11. Uncaring; uninterested
13. Horrible; abominable; reprehensible
14. Repulsive; disgusting; offensive
16. Japanese money
17. People devoted to pleasure and luxury
18. Book containing hymns and prayers
19. Worn out; broken down from use

### Down
2. Stopping and starting at intervals
3. Feeling of embarrassment or humiliation caused by failure or disappointment
4. Producing the desired effect
6. Short and to the point
7. Of or containing chemicals that cause fire when exploded
8. Poisonous atmosphere
9. Exploration of an area to gather information
12. Sudden outburst
13. Characterized by the pursuit of sensual pleasure
15. Scorched

# Hiroshima Vocabulary Crossword 4

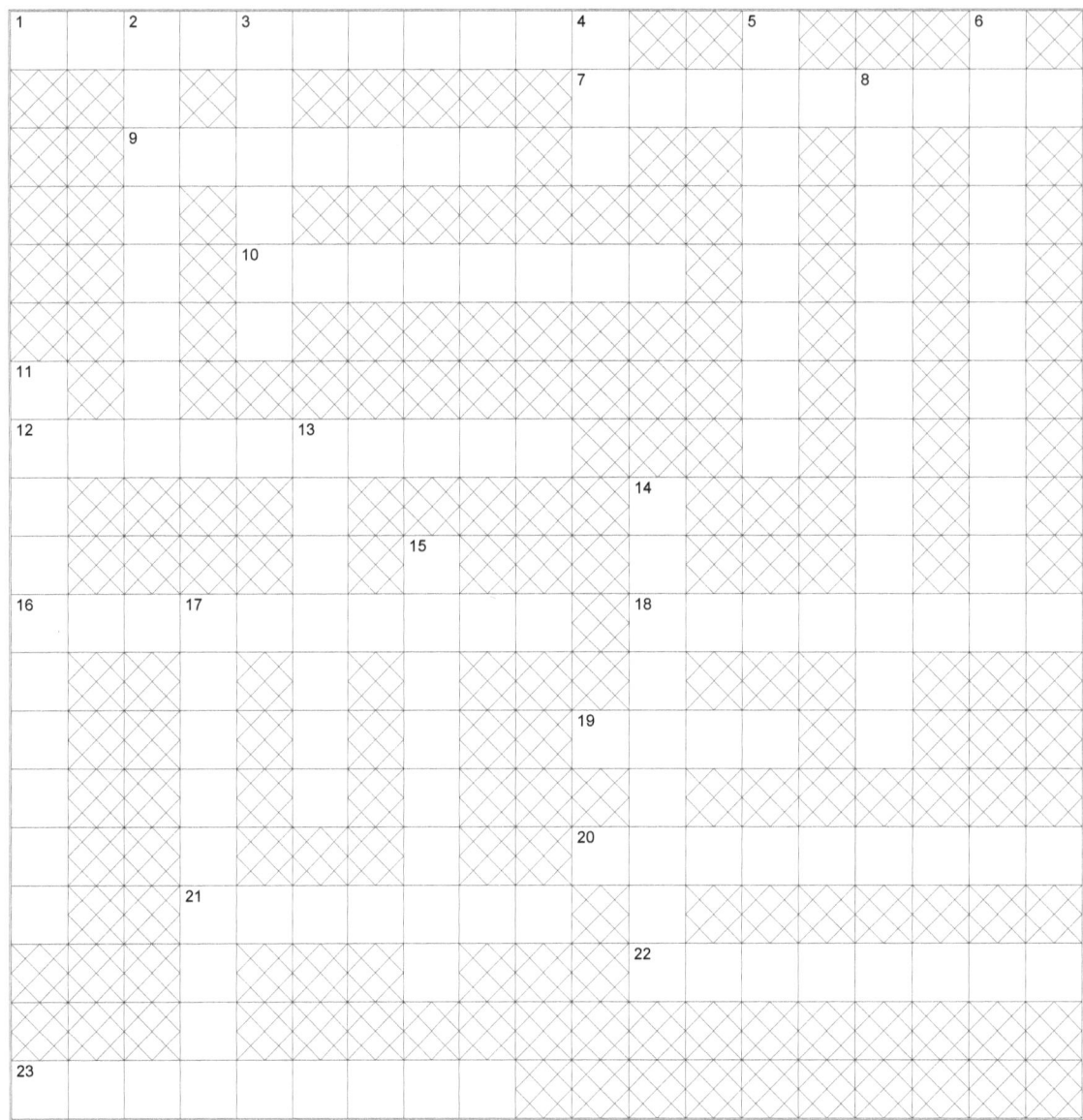

**Across**
1. Basic; at the roots
7. Producing the desired effect
9. Feeling of embarrassment or humiliation caused by failure or disappointment
10. About to die
12. Pulled out
16. Dangerously lacking in security or stability
18. Forced; battered
19. Basic, central, or critical point
20. Return of a trait after a period of absence
21. Horrible; abominable; reprehensible
22. Short and to the point
23. Uncaring; uninterested

**Down**
2. Worn out; broken down from use
3. Poisonous atmosphere
4. Japanese money
5. Sudden outburst
6. Decomposed, rotten, foul-smelling matter
8. Stopping and starting at intervals
11. Having a fear of foreigners
13. Scorched
14. People devoted to pleasure and luxury
15. Conscious decision
17. One who teaches Christian doctrines

Hiroshima Vocabulary Crossword 4 Answer Key

**Across**
1. Basic; at the roots
7. Producing the desired effect
9. Feeling of embarrassment or humiliation caused by failure or disappointment
10. About to die
12. Pulled out
16. Dangerously lacking in security or stability
18. Forced; battered
19. Basic, central, or critical point
20. Return of a trait after a period of absence
21. Horrible; abominable; reprehensible
22. Short and to the point
23. Uncaring; uninterested

**Down**
2. Worn out; broken down from use
3. Poisonous atmosphere
4. Japanese money
5. Sudden outburst
6. Decomposed, rotten, foul-smelling matter
8. Stopping and starting at intervals
11. Having a fear of foreigners
13. Scorched
14. People devoted to pleasure and luxury
15. Conscious decision
17. One who teaches Christian doctrines

Hiroshima Vocabulary Juggle Letters 1

1. SOAERTCENC = 1. _____
   Make sacred

2. EIOHSUN = 2. _____
   Horrible; abominable; reprehensible

3. STCIIOSULO = 3. _____
   Marked by anxious care and attentiveness

4. MNAEAOITN = 4. _____
   Something coming forth from a source

5. HCRDERA = 5. _____
   Scorched

6. TCXIREATED = 6. _____
   Pulled out

7. SODNITHICE = 7. _____
   Characterized by the pursuit of sensual pleasure

8. YRSBEASTI = 8. _____
   People devoted to pleasure and luxury

9. DUSPETIEF = 9. _____
   With senses dulled by amazement

10. FTLECARERPU = 10. _____
    District administered or governed by a prefect

11. SNOYLSTBEI = 11. _____
    Represented or appearing as such

12. ALIACMISTN = 12. _____
    Magical

13. TAZNIUGIDTTIIN = 13. _____
    Assuming a false attitude; posturing

14. NEY = 14. _____
    Japanese money

15. SMLEAIA = 15. _____
    Sense of bodily discomfort, depression, or unease

Hiroshima Vocabulary Juggle Letters 1 Answer Key

1. SOAERTCENC = 1. CONSECRATE
   Make sacred

2. EIOHSUN = 2. HEINOUS
   Horrible; abominable; reprehensible

3. STCIIOSULO = 3. SOLICITOUS
   Marked by anxious care and attentiveness

4. MNAEAOITN = 4. EMANATION
   Something coming forth from a source

5. HCRDERA = 5. CHARRED
   Scorched

6. TCXIREATED = 6. EXTRICATED
   Pulled out

7. SODNITHICE = 7. HEDONISTIC
   Characterized by the pursuit of sensual pleasure

8. YRSBEASTI = 8. SYBARITES
   People devoted to pleasure and luxury

9. DUSPETIEF = 9. STUPEFIED
   With senses dulled by amazement

10. FTLECARERPU = 10. PREFECTURAL
    District administered or governed by a prefect

11. SNOYLSTBEI = 11. OSTENSIBLY
    Represented or appearing as such

12. ALIACMISTN = 12. TALISMANIC
    Magical

13. TAZNIUGIDTTIIN = 13. ATTITUDINIZING
    Assuming a false attitude; posturing

14. NEY = 14. YEN
    Japanese money

15. SMLEAIA = 15. MALAISE
    Sense of bodily discomfort, depression, or unease

Hiroshima Vocabulary Juggle Letters 2

1. RUDOBIMN = 1. _____
   About to die

2. POHBXCINOE = 2. _____
   Having a fear of foreigners

3. ROUSICPICA = 3. _____
   Unpredictable

4. RACIGNH = 4. _____
   Feeling of embarrassment or humiliation caused by failure or disappointment

5. GRUNNETPA = 5. _____
   Repulsive; disgusting; offensive

6. NEY = 6. _____
   Japanese money

7. NOTEDHICSI = 7. _____
   Characterized by the pursuit of sensual pleasure

8. RTCEIETDAX = 8. _____
   Pulled out

9. NUZTIDTTIIAIGN = 9. _____
   Assuming a false attitude; posturing

10. STSNUINOOC =10. _____
    Bruises

11. TEATIAHPC =11. _____
    Uncaring; uninterested

12. SICALMNAIT =12. _____
    Magical

13. REBRVAIY =13. _____
    Book containing hymns and prayers

14. IFFCUASOE =14. _____
    Producing the desired effect

15. DPPAETRUSU =15. _____
    Full of pus

Hiroshima Vocabulary Juggle Letters 2 Answer Key

1. RUDOBIMN = 1. MORIBUND
About to die

2. POHBXCINOE = 2. XENOPHOBIC
Having a fear of foreigners

3. ROUSICPICA = 3. CAPRICIOUS
Unpredictable

4. RACIGNH = 4. CHAGRIN
Feeling of embarrassment or humiliation caused by failure or disappointment

5. GRUNNETPA = 5. REPUGNANT
Repulsive; disgusting; offensive

6. NEY = 6. YEN
Japanese money

7. NOTEDHICSI = 7. HEDONISTIC
Characterized by the pursuit of sensual pleasure

8. RTCEIETDAX = 8. EXTRICATED
Pulled out

9. NUZTIDTTIIAIGN = 9. ATTITUDINIZING
Assuming a false attitude; posturing

10. STSNUINOOC = 10. CONTUSIONS
Bruises

11. TEATIAHPC = 11. APATHETIC
Uncaring; uninterested

12. SICALMNAIT = 12. TALISMANIC
Magical

13. REBRVAIY = 13. BREVIARY
Book containing hymns and prayers

14. IFFCUASOE = 14. EFFACIOUS
Producing the desired effect

15. DPPAETRUSU = 15. SUPPURATED
Full of pus

Hiroshima Vocabulary Juggle Letters 3

1. DESTCIOHNI = 1. _____
   Characterized by the pursuit of sensual pleasure

2. FEDBUTEF = 2. _____
   Forced; battered

3. PICEDETR = 3. _____
   Worn out; broken down from use

4. AOIUSRPCCI = 4. _____
   Unpredictable

5. TTNIGDTIZIAUNI = 5. _____
   Assuming a false attitude; posturing

6. ONISNTOUCS = 6. _____
   Bruises

7. TCCIUSNC = 7. _____
   Short and to the point

8. MNSAICAITL = 8. _____
   Magical

9. OVTNIILO = 9. _____
   Conscious decision

10. ODLPMEEM = 10. _____
    Beat; hit

11. MRYRADIUNTE = 11. _____
    Basic; at the roots

12. ENY = 12. _____
    Japanese money

13. RRCEAHD = 13. _____
    Scorched

14. PTIEHATCA = 14. _____
    Uncaring; uninterested

15. SATBIRSYE = 15. _____
    People devoted to pleasure and luxury

Hiroshima Vocabulary Juggle Letters 3 Answer Key

1. DESTCIOHNI = 1. HEDONISTIC
Characterized by the pursuit of sensual pleasure

2. FEDBUTEF = 2. BUFFETED
Forced; battered

3. PICEDETR = 3. DECREPIT
Worn out; broken down from use

4. AOIUSRPCCI = 4. CAPRICIOUS
Unpredictable

5. TTNIGDTIZIAUNI = 5. ATTITUDINIZING
Assuming a false attitude; posturing

6. ONISNTOUCS = 6. CONTUSIONS
Bruises

7. TCCIUSNC = 7. SUCCINCT
Short and to the point

8. MNSAICAITL = 8. TALISMANIC
Magical

9. OVTNIILO = 9. VOLITION
Conscious decision

10. ODLPMEEM = 10. POMMELED
Beat; hit

11. MRYRADIUNTE = 11. RUDIMENTARY
Basic; at the roots

12. ENY = 12. YEN
Japanese money

13. RRCEAHD = 13. CHARRED
Scorched

14. PTIEHATCA = 14. APATHETIC
Uncaring; uninterested

15. SATBIRSYE = 15. SYBARITES
People devoted to pleasure and luxury

Hiroshima Vocabulary Juggle Letters 4

1. BSRIYSTEA = 1. _____
   People devoted to pleasure and luxury

2. TLANMIASCI = 2. _____
   Magical

3. HACIEAPTT = 3. _____
   Uncaring; uninterested

4. EDTIRECXAT = 4. _____
   Pulled out

5. CASERNECOT = 5. _____
   Make sacred

6. AERDCRH = 6. _____
   Scorched

7. LASEIMA = 7. _____
   Sense of bodily discomfort, depression, or unease

8. FUELAEPTCRR = 8. _____
   District administered or governed by a prefect

9. DTUITNIITGNIAZ = 9. _____
   Assuming a false attitude; posturing

10. RAUCPEROSI = 10. _____
    Dangerously lacking in security or stability

11. TIIACTSAV = 11. _____
    Return of a trait after a period of absence

12. EUTNRNGAP = 12. _____
    Repulsive; disgusting; offensive

13. CREESUNETCP = 13. _____
    Decomposed, rotten, foul-smelling matter

14. ANDYRCINEI = 14. _____
    Of or containing chemicals that cause fire when exploded

15. OIHNOBPXCE = 15. _____
    Having a fear of foreigners

Hiroshima Vocabulary Juggle Letters 4 Answer Key

1. BSRIYSTEA = 1. SYBARITES
People devoted to pleasure and luxury

2. TLANMIASCI = 2. TALISMANIC
Magical

3. HACIEAPTT = 3. APATHETIC
Uncaring; uninterested

4. EDTIRECXAT = 4. EXTRICATED
Pulled out

5. CASERNECOT = 5. CONSECRATE
Make sacred

6. AERDCRH = 6. CHARRED
Scorched

7. LASEIMA = 7. MALAISE
Sense of bodily discomfort, depression, or unease

8. FUELAEPTCRR = 8. PREFECTURAL
District administered or governed by a prefect

9. DTUITNIITGNIAZ = 9. ATTITUDINIZING
Assuming a false attitude; posturing

10. RAUCPEROSI =10. PRECARIOUS
Dangerously lacking in security or stability

11. TIIACTSAV =11. ATAVISTIC
Return of a trait after a period of absence

12. EUTNRNGAP =12. REPUGNANT
Repulsive; disgusting; offensive

13. CREESUNETCP =13. PUTRESCENCE
Decomposed, rotten, foul-smelling matter

14. ANDYRCINEI =14. INCENDIARY
Of or containing chemicals that cause fire when exploded

15. OIHNOBPXCE =15. XENOPHOBIC
Having a fear of foreigners

Copyrighted

| | |
|---|---|
| APATHETIC | Uncaring; uninterested |
| ATAVISTIC | Return of a trait after a period of absence |
| ATTITUDINIZING | Assuming a false attitude; posturing |
| BREVIARY | Book containing hymns and prayers |
| BUFFETED | Forced; battered |
| CAPRICIOUS | Unpredictable |

| | |
|---|---|
| CATECHIST | One who teaches Christian doctrines |
| CHAGRIN | Feeling of embarrassment or humiliation caused by failure or disappointment |
| CHARRED | Scorched |
| CONSECRATE | Make sacred |
| CONTUSIONS | Bruises |
| CONVIVIAL | Sociable |

| CRUX | Basic, central, or critical point |
| --- | --- |
| DECREPIT | Worn out; broken down from use |
| EFFACIOUS | Producing the desired effect |
| EMANATION | Something coming forth from a source |
| EXTRICATED | Pulled out |
| HEDONISTIC | Characterized by the pursuit of sensual pleasure |

| | |
|---|---|
| HEINOUS | Horrible; abominable; reprehensible |
| INCENDIARY | Of or containing chemicals that cause fire when exploded |
| INTERMITTENT | Stopping and starting at intervals |
| MALAISE | Sense of bodily discomfort, depression, or unease |
| MIASMA | Poisonous atmosphere |
| MORIBUND | About to die |

| | |
|---|---|
| OSTENSIBLY | Represented or appearing as such |
| PAROXYSM | Sudden outburst |
| POMMELED | Beat; hit |
| PRECARIOUS | Dangerously lacking in security or stability |
| PREFECTURAL | District administered or governed by a prefect |
| PUTRESCENCE | Decomposed, rotten, foul-smelling matter |

| | |
|---|---|
| RECONNAISSANCE | Exploration of an area to gather information |
| REPUGNANT | Repulsive; disgusting; offensive |
| RUDIMENTARY | Basic; at the roots |
| SOLICITOUS | Marked by anxious care and attentiveness |
| STUPEFIED | With senses dulled by amazement |
| SUCCINCT | Short and to the point |

| | |
|---|---|
| SUPPURATED | Full of pus |
| SYBARITES | People devoted to pleasure and luxury |
| TALISMANIC | Magical |
| VOLITION | Conscious decision |
| XENOPHOBIC | Having a fear of foreigners |
| YEN | Japanese money |

## Hiroshima Vocabulary

| PAROXYSM | TALISMANIC | APATHETIC | MALAISE | HEINOUS |
|---|---|---|---|---|
| SYBARITES | PUTRESCENCE | VOLITION | SUPPURATED | OSTENSIBLY |
| REPUGNANT | BREVIARY | FREE SPACE | MORIBUND | STUPEFIED |
| EXTRICATED | DECREPIT | EMANATION | PRECARIOUS | YEN |
| PREFECTURAL | ATAVISTIC | CONTUSIONS | SUCCINCT | CATECHIST |

## Hiroshima Vocabulary

| CONSECRATE | SOLICITOUS | RECONNAISSANCE | BUFFETED | CHARRED |
|---|---|---|---|---|
| POMMELED | CAPRICIOUS | INCENDIARY | EFFACIOUS | INTERMITTENT |
| CRUX | CHAGRIN | FREE SPACE | HEDONISTIC | ATTITUDINIZING |
| CONVIVIAL | XENOPHOBIC | CATECHIST | SUCCINCT | CONTUSIONS |
| ATAVISTIC | PREFECTURAL | YEN | PRECARIOUS | EMANATION |

## Hiroshima Vocabulary

| CONVIVIAL | YEN | PREFECTURAL | CONSECRATE | CATECHIST |
|---|---|---|---|---|
| BREVIARY | CAPRICIOUS | XENOPHOBIC | MORIBUND | CHARRED |
| SOLICITOUS | EMANATION | FREE SPACE | HEINOUS | RUDIMENTARY |
| EXTRICATED | OSTENSIBLY | BUFFETED | TALISMANIC | SUCCINCT |
| MALAISE | INCENDIARY | PAROXYSM | STUPEFIED | SUPPURATED |

## Hiroshima Vocabulary

| INTERMITTENT | SYBARITES | DECREPIT | APATHETIC | PRECARIOUS |
|---|---|---|---|---|
| CONTUSIONS | VOLITION | REPUGNANT | CHAGRIN | MIASMA |
| HEDONISTIC | ATTITUDINIZING | FREE SPACE | CRUX | EFFACIOUS |
| ATAVISTIC | RECONNAISSANCE | SUPPURATED | STUPEFIED | PAROXYSM |
| INCENDIARY | MALAISE | SUCCINCT | TALISMANIC | BUFFETED |

Hiroshima Vocabulary

| BREVIARY | EFFACIOUS | INTERMITTENT | PUTRESCENCE | SUPPURATED |
|---|---|---|---|---|
| EXTRICATED | RUDIMENTARY | CRUX | CAPRICIOUS | MORIBUND |
| TALISMANIC | YEN | FREE SPACE | CONVIVIAL | EMANATION |
| PREFECTURAL | DECREPIT | CHARRED | CONSECRATE | XENOPHOBIC |
| POMMELED | CONTUSIONS | OSTENSIBLY | PAROXYSM | PRECARIOUS |

Hiroshima Vocabulary

| CATECHIST | STUPEFIED | ATAVISTIC | MALAISE | APATHETIC |
|---|---|---|---|---|
| SYBARITES | VOLITION | INCENDIARY | SOLICITOUS | BUFFETED |
| CHAGRIN | RECONNAISSANCE | FREE SPACE | SUCCINCT | HEINOUS |
| ATTITUDINIZING | REPUGNANT | PRECARIOUS | PAROXYSM | OSTENSIBLY |
| CONTUSIONS | POMMELED | XENOPHOBIC | CONSECRATE | CHARRED |

Hiroshima Vocabulary

| SUCCINCT | YEN | SUPPURATED | TALISMANIC | PRECARIOUS |
|---|---|---|---|---|
| BUFFETED | PUTRESCENCE | CHARRED | INCENDIARY | OSTENSIBLY |
| POMMELED | MIASMA | FREE SPACE | RUDIMENTARY | HEDONISTIC |
| ATAVISTIC | STUPEFIED | ATTITUDINIZING | EMANATION | CONVIVIAL |
| CATECHIST | MALAISE | BREVIARY | MORIBUND | EXTRICATED |

Hiroshima Vocabulary

| CRUX | CAPRICIOUS | HEINOUS | INTERMITTENT | APATHETIC |
|---|---|---|---|---|
| VOLITION | CONSECRATE | CONTUSIONS | SOLICITOUS | XENOPHOBIC |
| RECONNAISSANCE | PAROXYSM | FREE SPACE | SYBARITES | REPUGNANT |
| DECREPIT | EFFACIOUS | EXTRICATED | MORIBUND | BREVIARY |
| MALAISE | CATECHIST | CONVIVIAL | EMANATION | ATTITUDINIZING |

## Hiroshima Vocabulary

| CONVIVIAL | STUPEFIED | CONTUSIONS | INCENDIARY | SOLICITOUS |
|---|---|---|---|---|
| CATECHIST | HEINOUS | REPUGNANT | CRUX | MALAISE |
| EMANATION | CHARRED | FREE SPACE | SUPPURATED | CAPRICIOUS |
| CHAGRIN | OSTENSIBLY | ATTITUDINIZING | RUDIMENTARY | TALISMANIC |
| PREFECTURAL | VOLITION | CONSECRATE | XENOPHOBIC | POMMELED |

## Hiroshima Vocabulary

| PAROXYSM | APATHETIC | BUFFETED | BREVIARY | HEDONISTIC |
|---|---|---|---|---|
| RECONNAISSANCE | EXTRICATED | PRECARIOUS | MIASMA | SUCCINCT |
| ATAVISTIC | MORIBUND | FREE SPACE | INTERMITTENT | SYBARITES |
| EFFACIOUS | YEN | POMMELED | XENOPHOBIC | CONSECRATE |
| VOLITION | PREFECTURAL | TALISMANIC | RUDIMENTARY | ATTITUDINIZING |

## Hiroshima Vocabulary

| ATAVISTIC | PREFECTURAL | DECREPIT | HEINOUS | ATTITUDINIZING |
|---|---|---|---|---|
| INCENDIARY | SUCCINCT | INTERMITTENT | CHAGRIN | MIASMA |
| CHARRED | PUTRESCENCE | FREE SPACE | BREVIARY | SUPPURATED |
| REPUGNANT | APATHETIC | BUFFETED | CONTUSIONS | EMANATION |
| CONVIVIAL | HEDONISTIC | VOLITION | EXTRICATED | PRECARIOUS |

## Hiroshima Vocabulary

| STUPEFIED | MALAISE | EFFACIOUS | OSTENSIBLY | PAROXYSM |
|---|---|---|---|---|
| POMMELED | RECONNAISSANCE | CONSECRATE | CAPRICIOUS | MORIBUND |
| RUDIMENTARY | XENOPHOBIC | FREE SPACE | CRUX | SYBARITES |
| TALISMANIC | SOLICITOUS | PRECARIOUS | EXTRICATED | VOLITION |
| HEDONISTIC | CONVIVIAL | EMANATION | CONTUSIONS | BUFFETED |

## Hiroshima Vocabulary

| EFFACIOUS | VOLITION | PRECARIOUS | APATHETIC | EXTRICATED |
|---|---|---|---|---|
| POMMELED | CATECHIST | HEDONISTIC | RECONNAISSANCE | PAROXYSM |
| CHARRED | MALAISE | FREE SPACE | BUFFETED | DECREPIT |
| MIASMA | CONTUSIONS | STUPEFIED | CRUX | PREFECTURAL |
| CONSECRATE | INTERMITTENT | ATAVISTIC | XENOPHOBIC | OSTENSIBLY |

## Hiroshima Vocabulary

| REPUGNANT | CHAGRIN | PUTRESCENCE | YEN | CAPRICIOUS |
|---|---|---|---|---|
| ATTITUDINIZING | SUPPURATED | INCENDIARY | RUDIMENTARY | HEINOUS |
| SYBARITES | TALISMANIC | FREE SPACE | EMANATION | BREVIARY |
| MORIBUND | CONVIVIAL | OSTENSIBLY | XENOPHOBIC | ATAVISTIC |
| INTERMITTENT | CONSECRATE | PREFECTURAL | CRUX | STUPEFIED |

Hiroshima Vocabulary

| EXTRICATED | VOLITION | CAPRICIOUS | INTERMITTENT | DECREPIT |
|---|---|---|---|---|
| RECONNAISSANCE | POMMELED | ATTITUDINIZING | BUFFETED | CRUX |
| REPUGNANT | PREFECTURAL | FREE SPACE | PUTRESCENCE | PAROXYSM |
| RUDIMENTARY | SYBARITES | SUPPURATED | SUCCINCT | CONTUSIONS |
| PRECARIOUS | ATAVISTIC | BREVIARY | CATECHIST | SOLICITOUS |

Hiroshima Vocabulary

| CHARRED | APATHETIC | XENOPHOBIC | HEDONISTIC | STUPEFIED |
|---|---|---|---|---|
| EFFACIOUS | YEN | MORIBUND | CONVIVIAL | OSTENSIBLY |
| INCENDIARY | HEINOUS | FREE SPACE | CHAGRIN | TALISMANIC |
| CONSECRATE | MALAISE | SOLICITOUS | CATECHIST | BREVIARY |
| ATAVISTIC | PRECARIOUS | CONTUSIONS | SUCCINCT | SUPPURATED |

## Hiroshima Vocabulary

| CONTUSIONS | INTERMITTENT | YEN | XENOPHOBIC | CRUX |
|---|---|---|---|---|
| CONSECRATE | ATTITUDINIZING | CONVIVIAL | PRECARIOUS | OSTENSIBLY |
| INCENDIARY | RUDIMENTARY | FREE SPACE | MIASMA | CAPRICIOUS |
| SUPPURATED | EXTRICATED | STUPEFIED | POMMELED | PREFECTURAL |
| DECREPIT | VOLITION | CHARRED | PAROXYSM | PUTRESCENCE |

## Hiroshima Vocabulary

| TALISMANIC | SUCCINCT | BUFFETED | REPUGNANT | HEINOUS |
|---|---|---|---|---|
| CHAGRIN | HEDONISTIC | SYBARITES | EMANATION | SOLICITOUS |
| MORIBUND | BREVIARY | FREE SPACE | RECONNAISSANCE | EFFACIOUS |
| APATHETIC | MALAISE | PUTRESCENCE | PAROXYSM | CHARRED |
| VOLITION | DECREPIT | PREFECTURAL | POMMELED | STUPEFIED |

Hiroshima Vocabulary

| YEN | EFFACIOUS | HEINOUS | CRUX | REPUGNANT |
|---|---|---|---|---|
| PUTRESCENCE | CHAGRIN | HEDONISTIC | RECONNAISSANCE | TALISMANIC |
| SYBARITES | CATECHIST | FREE SPACE | SUCCINCT | CONTUSIONS |
| INTERMITTENT | INCENDIARY | CONSECRATE | SOLICITOUS | RUDIMENTARY |
| CONVIVIAL | PRECARIOUS | MIASMA | ATAVISTIC | BUFFETED |

Hiroshima Vocabulary

| DECREPIT | EXTRICATED | PREFECTURAL | POMMELED | APATHETIC |
|---|---|---|---|---|
| MALAISE | BREVIARY | VOLITION | ATTITUDINIZING | PAROXYSM |
| CAPRICIOUS | SUPPURATED | FREE SPACE | XENOPHOBIC | EMANATION |
| MORIBUND | CHARRED | BUFFETED | ATAVISTIC | MIASMA |
| PRECARIOUS | CONVIVIAL | RUDIMENTARY | SOLICITOUS | CONSECRATE |

## Hiroshima Vocabulary

| SYBARITES | BREVIARY | EFFACIOUS | PRECARIOUS | YEN |
|---|---|---|---|---|
| OSTENSIBLY | ATTITUDINIZING | MORIBUND | BUFFETED | CONTUSIONS |
| CAPRICIOUS | ATAVISTIC | FREE SPACE | INCENDIARY | HEDONISTIC |
| MALAISE | PREFECTURAL | VOLITION | APATHETIC | DECREPIT |
| SUPPURATED | HEINOUS | RECONNAISSANCE | PAROXYSM | MIASMA |

## Hiroshima Vocabulary

| POMMELED | XENOPHOBIC | TALISMANIC | EMANATION | PUTRESCENCE |
|---|---|---|---|---|
| INTERMITTENT | EXTRICATED | CONSECRATE | REPUGNANT | SUCCINCT |
| CHAGRIN | CHARRED | FREE SPACE | STUPEFIED | RUDIMENTARY |
| CATECHIST | CONVIVIAL | MIASMA | PAROXYSM | RECONNAISSANCE |
| HEINOUS | SUPPURATED | DECREPIT | APATHETIC | VOLITION |

Hiroshima Vocabulary

| INTERMITTENT | BREVIARY | TALISMANIC | EMANATION | RECONNAISSANCE |
|---|---|---|---|---|
| CONSECRATE | SYBARITES | RUDIMENTARY | EFFACIOUS | XENOPHOBIC |
| REPUGNANT | PRECARIOUS | FREE SPACE | CHARRED | SUCCINCT |
| INCENDIARY | CONVIVIAL | POMMELED | MORIBUND | CRUX |
| EXTRICATED | HEINOUS | HEDONISTIC | APATHETIC | PUTRESCENCE |

Hiroshima Vocabulary

| YEN | ATAVISTIC | MALAISE | DECREPIT | CAPRICIOUS |
|---|---|---|---|---|
| OSTENSIBLY | SOLICITOUS | VOLITION | ATTITUDINIZING | CHAGRIN |
| CONTUSIONS | STUPEFIED | FREE SPACE | BUFFETED | PAROXYSM |
| CATECHIST | SUPPURATED | PUTRESCENCE | APATHETIC | HEDONISTIC |
| HEINOUS | EXTRICATED | CRUX | MORIBUND | POMMELED |

## Hiroshima Vocabulary

| ATAVISTIC | SUCCINCT | CONVIVIAL | RECONNAISSANCE | HEDONISTIC |
|---|---|---|---|---|
| RUDIMENTARY | EFFACIOUS | PAROXYSM | CRUX | INTERMITTENT |
| MIASMA | PREFECTURAL | FREE SPACE | CONSECRATE | REPUGNANT |
| CAPRICIOUS | SYBARITES | CHAGRIN | APATHETIC | INCENDIARY |
| CATECHIST | MALAISE | CONTUSIONS | EMANATION | HEINOUS |

## Hiroshima Vocabulary

| SOLICITOUS | BREVIARY | DECREPIT | TALISMANIC | PRECARIOUS |
|---|---|---|---|---|
| BUFFETED | SUPPURATED | POMMELED | OSTENSIBLY | ATTITUDINIZING |
| EXTRICATED | PUTRESCENCE | FREE SPACE | STUPEFIED | YEN |
| XENOPHOBIC | MORIBUND | HEINOUS | EMANATION | CONTUSIONS |
| MALAISE | CATECHIST | INCENDIARY | APATHETIC | CHAGRIN |

Hiroshima Vocabulary

| CRUX | ATTITUDINIZING | CHARRED | DECREPIT | INCENDIARY |
|---|---|---|---|---|
| PUTRESCENCE | CONTUSIONS | OSTENSIBLY | ATAVISTIC | CHAGRIN |
| EMANATION | BREVIARY | FREE SPACE | CAPRICIOUS | SOLICITOUS |
| POMMELED | XENOPHOBIC | VOLITION | SYBARITES | CONVIVIAL |
| RUDIMENTARY | PREFECTURAL | SUCCINCT | CATECHIST | MORIBUND |

Hiroshima Vocabulary

| TALISMANIC | PAROXYSM | YEN | HEDONISTIC | BUFFETED |
|---|---|---|---|---|
| EXTRICATED | RECONNAISSANCE | MALAISE | STUPEFIED | APATHETIC |
| HEINOUS | CONSECRATE | FREE SPACE | REPUGNANT | SUPPURATED |
| PRECARIOUS | MIASMA | MORIBUND | CATECHIST | SUCCINCT |
| PREFECTURAL | RUDIMENTARY | CONVIVIAL | SYBARITES | VOLITION |

Hiroshima Vocabulary

| APATHETIC | RECONNAISSANCE | EMANATION | CHARRED | DECREPIT |
|---|---|---|---|---|
| CONVIVIAL | PRECARIOUS | VOLITION | EXTRICATED | TALISMANIC |
| INTERMITTENT | PREFECTURAL | FREE SPACE | BREVIARY | INCENDIARY |
| OSTENSIBLY | RUDIMENTARY | REPUGNANT | CRUX | CONTUSIONS |
| CHAGRIN | CONSECRATE | EFFACIOUS | SUCCINCT | PUTRESCENCE |

Hiroshima Vocabulary

| HEDONISTIC | HEINOUS | STUPEFIED | SYBARITES | SUPPURATED |
|---|---|---|---|---|
| MIASMA | MALAISE | XENOPHOBIC | CATECHIST | MORIBUND |
| ATAVISTIC | SOLICITOUS | FREE SPACE | YEN | BUFFETED |
| PAROXYSM | POMMELED | PUTRESCENCE | SUCCINCT | EFFACIOUS |
| CONSECRATE | CHAGRIN | CONTUSIONS | CRUX | REPUGNANT |

Hiroshima Vocabulary

| OSTENSIBLY | TALISMANIC | MORIBUND | EXTRICATED | RUDIMENTARY |
|---|---|---|---|---|
| SYBARITES | PREFECTURAL | STUPEFIED | PRECARIOUS | DECREPIT |
| CONSECRATE | MALAISE | FREE SPACE | CAPRICIOUS | HEINOUS |
| INCENDIARY | PUTRESCENCE | ATAVISTIC | SUPPURATED | BUFFETED |
| CATECHIST | CHARRED | CRUX | VOLITION | RECONNAISSANCE |

Hiroshima Vocabulary

| PAROXYSM | SOLICITOUS | POMMELED | XENOPHOBIC | HEDONISTIC |
|---|---|---|---|---|
| BREVIARY | EMANATION | CONVIVIAL | MIASMA | EFFACIOUS |
| SUCCINCT | YEN | FREE SPACE | INTERMITTENT | APATHETIC |
| REPUGNANT | CONTUSIONS | RECONNAISSANCE | VOLITION | CRUX |
| CHARRED | CATECHIST | BUFFETED | SUPPURATED | ATAVISTIC |

www.ingramcontent.com/pod-product-compliance
Lightning Source LLC
LaVergne TN
LVHW081538060526
838200LV00048B/2127